Queens of the Stone Age
Lullabies to Paralyze

Published by
Wise Publications,
8/9 Frith Street, London, W1D 3JB, England.

Exclusive distributors:
Music Sales Limited,
Distribution Centre, Newmarket Road, Bury St Edmunds,
Suffolk, IP33 3YB, England.

Music Sales Pty Limited,
120 Rothschild Avenue, Rosebery,
NSW 2018, Australia.

Order No. AM982916
ISBN 1-84609-065-2
This book © Copyright 2005 by Wise Publications,
a division of Music Sales Limited.

Music arrangements by Martin Shellard.
Music processed by Paul Ewers Music Design.
Edited by David Weston.
Original Art Design/Layout & Documentation by Hutch.
Illustrators - Keith Richards and Doug Cunningham.
Studio Photography by Nigel Copp.
Photographs by Chapman Baehler.
Printed in the United Kingdom.

www.musicsales.com

Your Guarantee of Quality:
As publishers, we strive to produce every book
to the highest commercial standards.

The music has been freshly engraved and the book has been
carefully designed to minimise awkward page turns and to make
playing from it a real pleasure. Particular care has been given
to opooifying acid-free, neutral-sized paper made from pulps
which have not been elemental chlorine bleached.

This pulp is from farmed sustainable forests
and was produced with special regard for the environment.

Throughout, the printing and binding have been planned to ensure a sturdy,
attractive publication which should give years of enjoyment.

If your copy fails to meet our high standards, please inform us
and we will gladly replace it.

DISTRIBUTED BY
HAL LEONARD
CORPORATION MILWAUKEE, WI 53213

THIS LULLABY

Words & Music by Josh Homme, Mark Lanegan, Joey Castillo & Troy Van Leeuwen

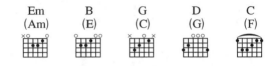

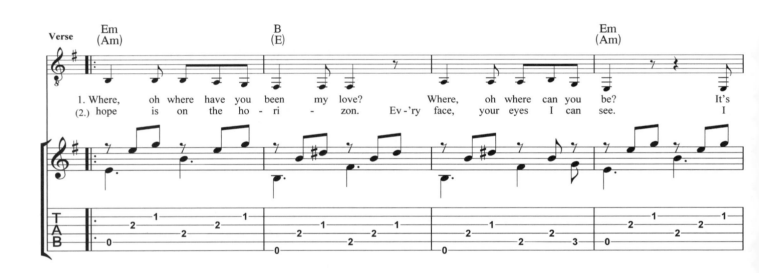

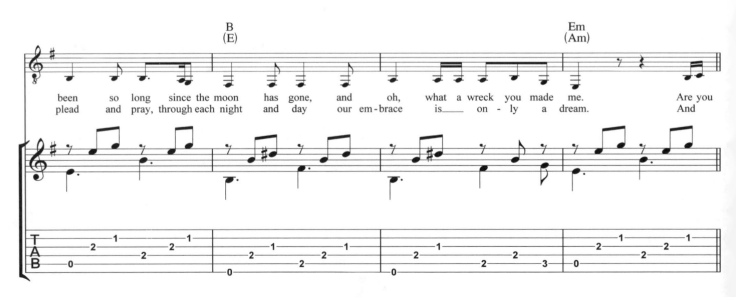

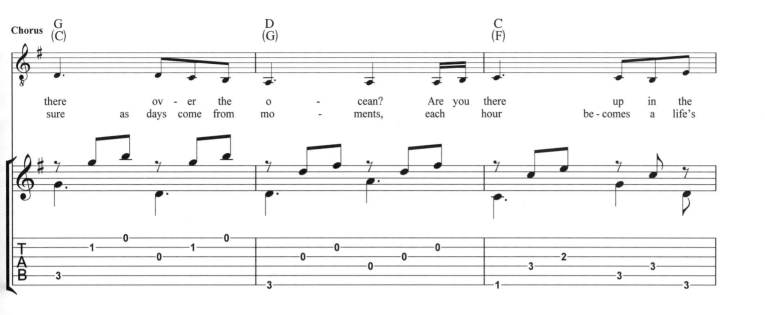

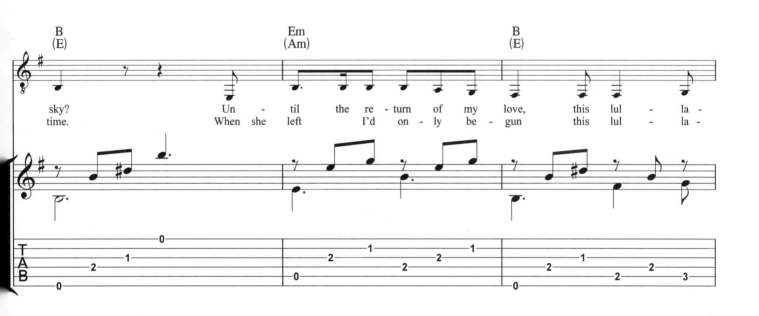

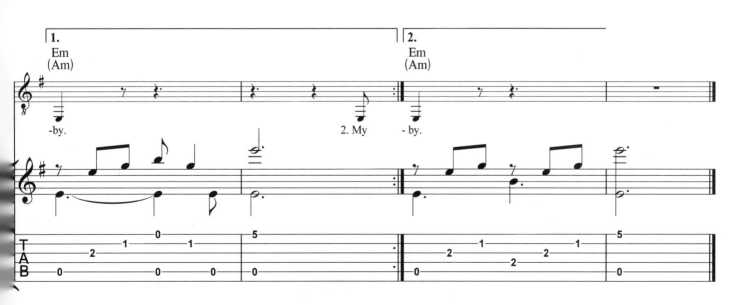

MEDICATION

Words & Music by Josh Homme, Joey Castillo & Troy Van Leeuwen

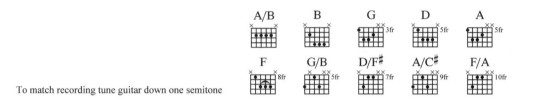

To match recording tune guitar down one semitone

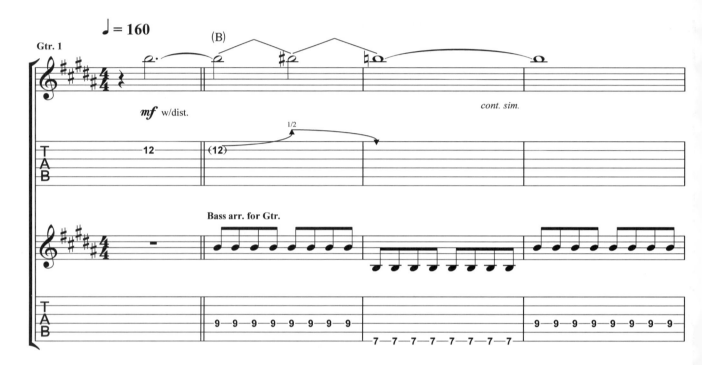

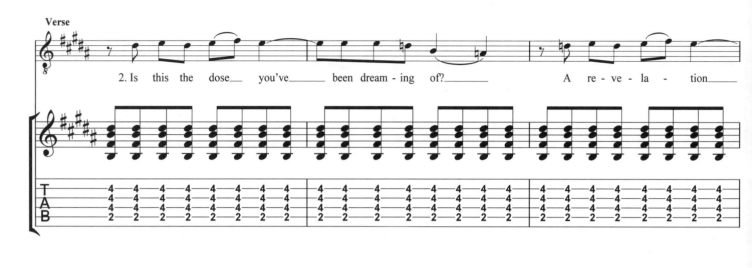

Verse

2. Is this the dose you've been dream-ing of? A re-ve-la - tion

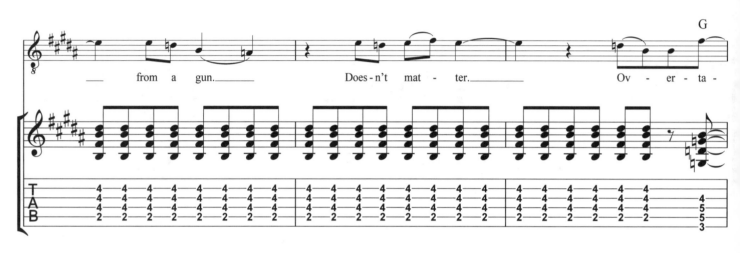

_ from a gun. Does-n't mat - ter. Ov - er - ta-

G

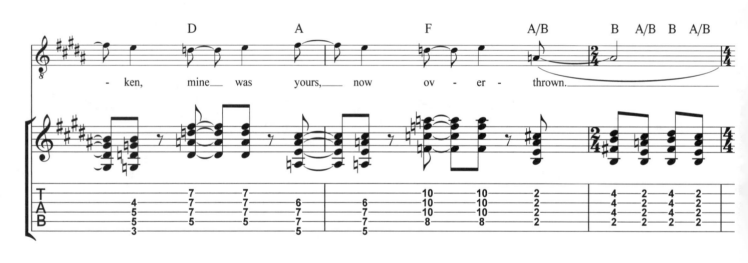

- ken, mine was yours, now ov - er - thrown.

D   A   F   A/B   B A/B B A/B

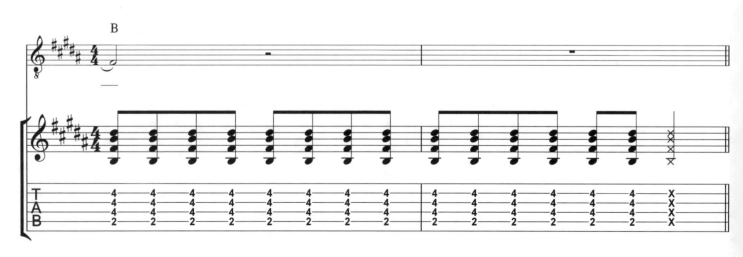

B

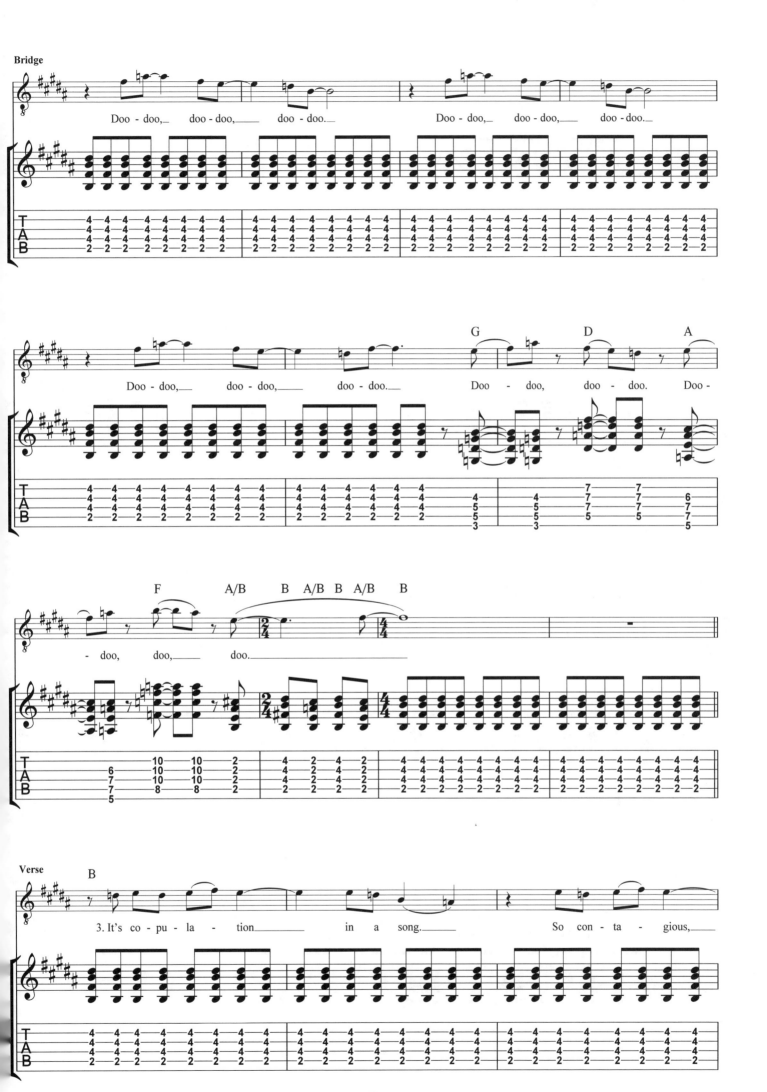

9

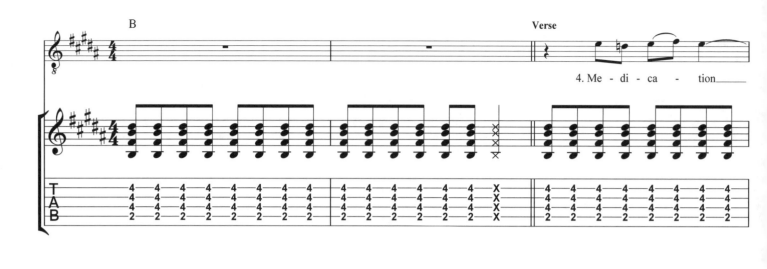

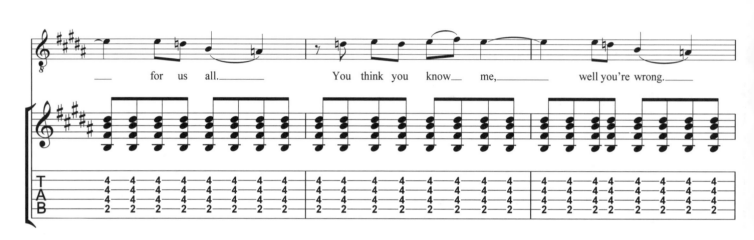

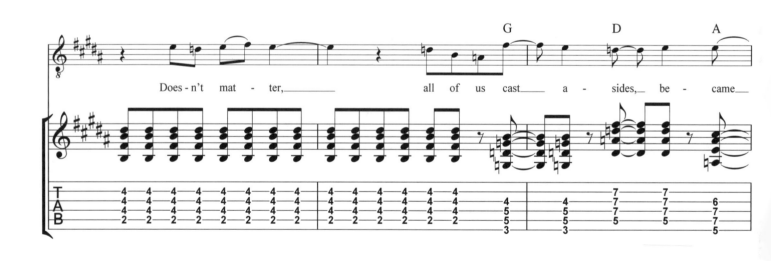

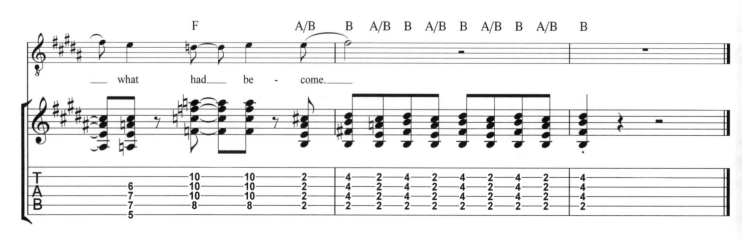

Everybody Knows That You Are Insane

Words & Music by Josh Homme, Joey Castillo & Troy Van Leeuwen

1. You wan - na know — why you
2. You're miss - ing out? Well

feel so hol - low? 'Cos you are.
if you say so. Then you're miss - ing out

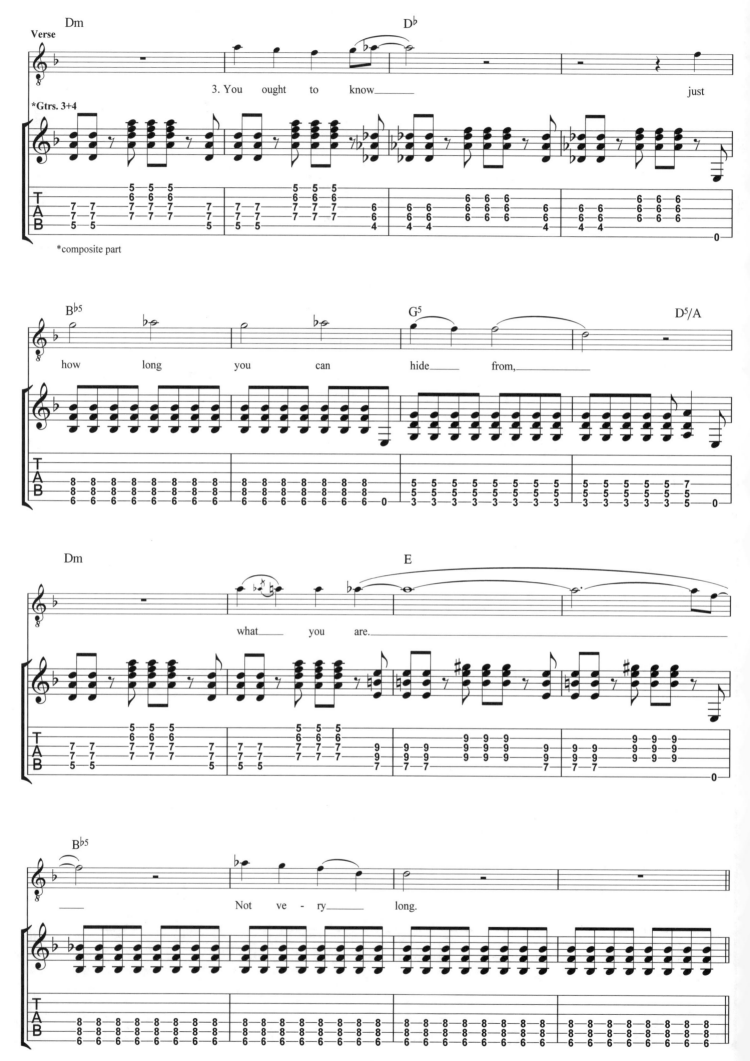

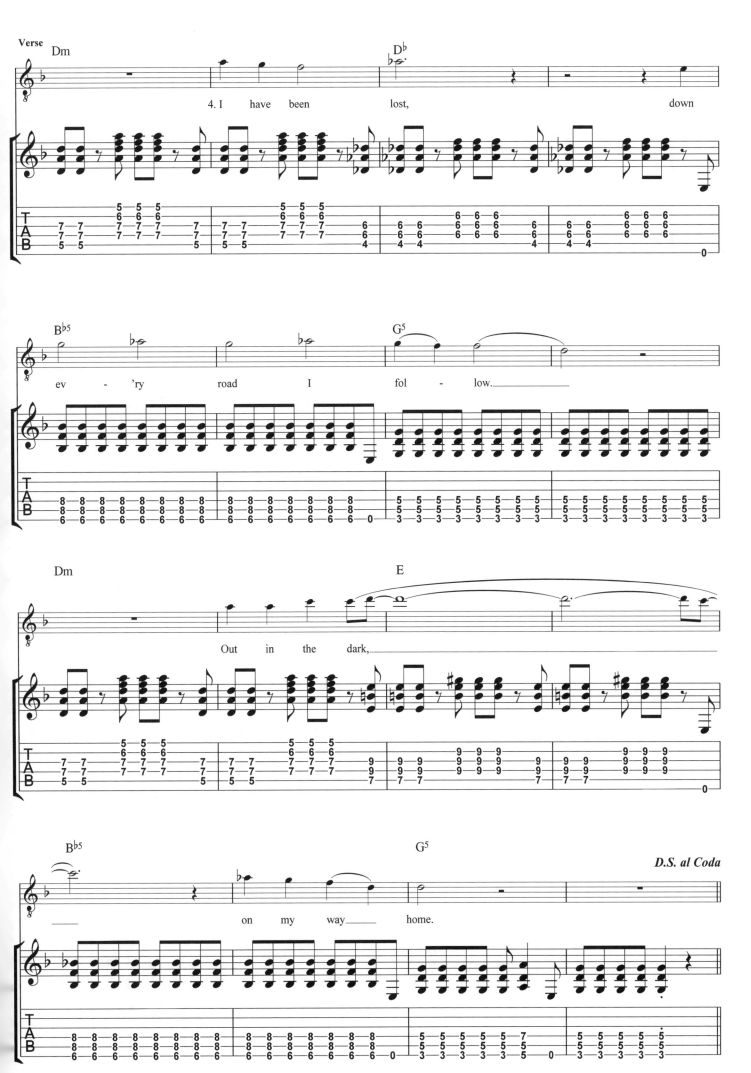

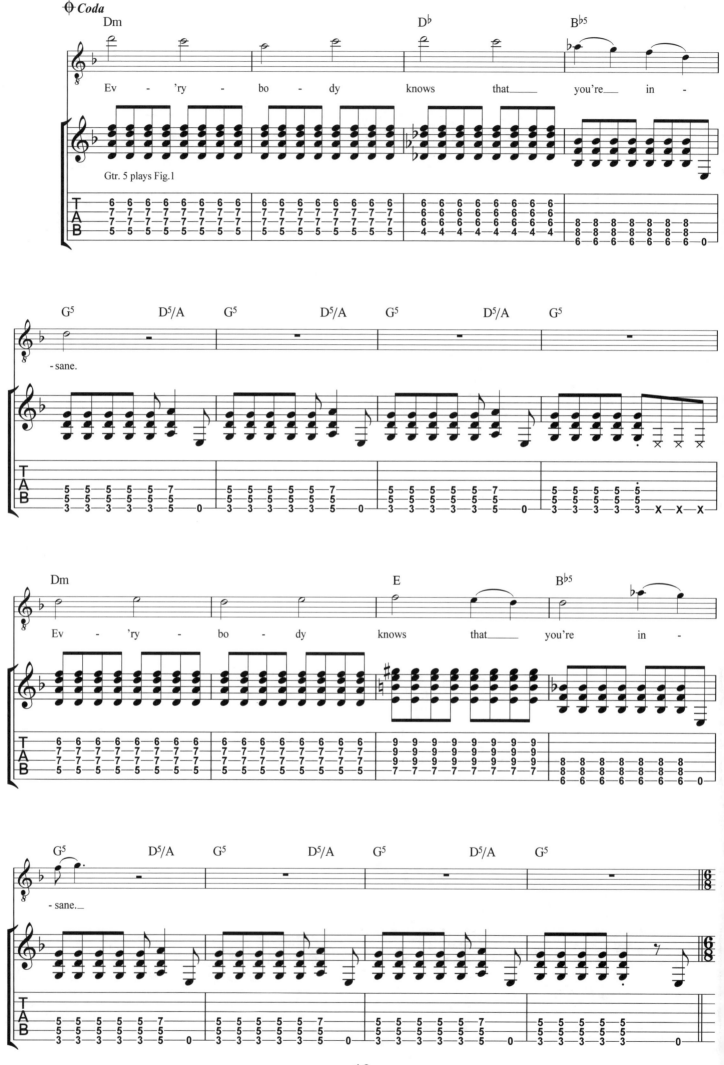

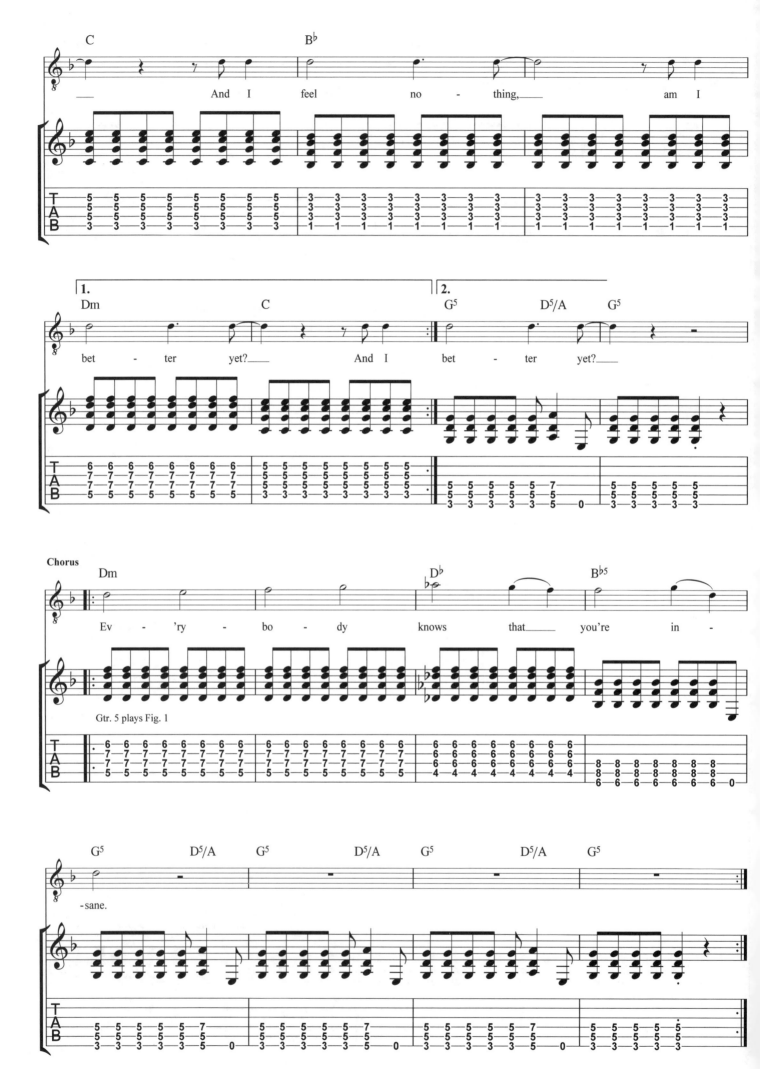

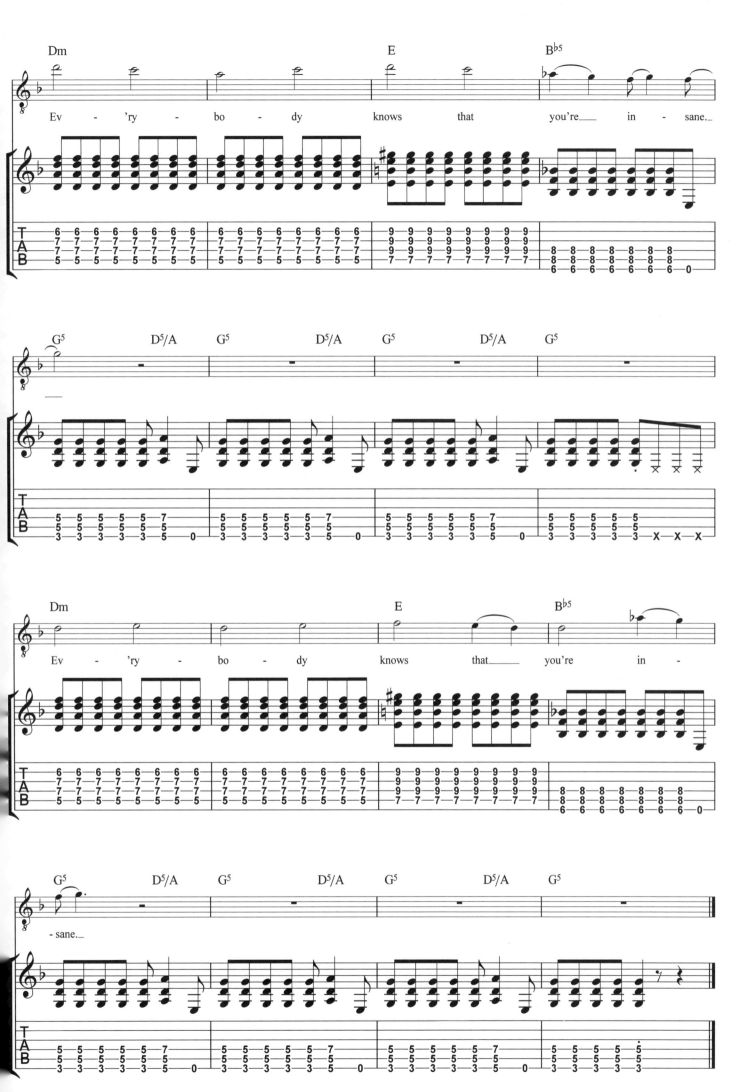

TANGLED UP IN PLAID

Words & Music by Josh Homme, Mark Lanegan, Joey Castillo & Troy Van Leeuwen

24

25

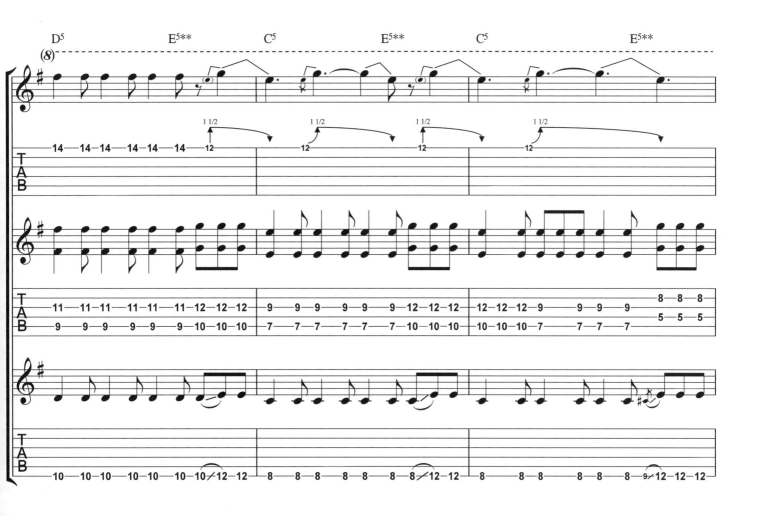

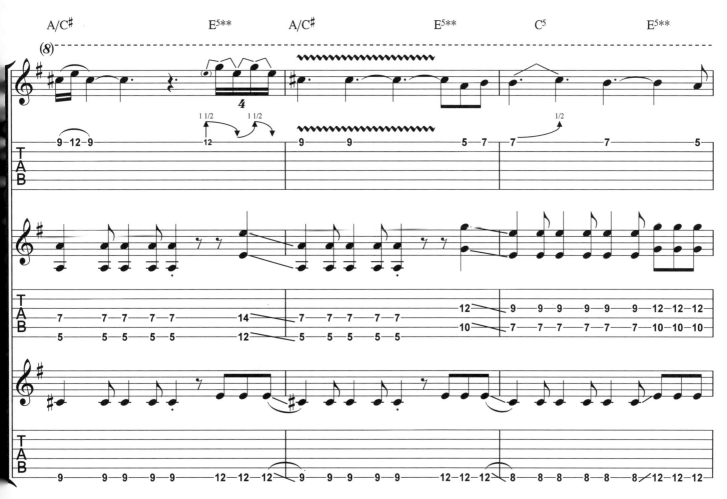

BURN THE WITCH

Words & Music by Josh Homme, Joey Castillo & Troy Van Leeuwen

*chords implied by harmony

31

* Pluck top note with second finger (*m*)

Verse

E⁵

3. Hold - ing hands,_____ skip - ping like a

Gtrs. 1+2

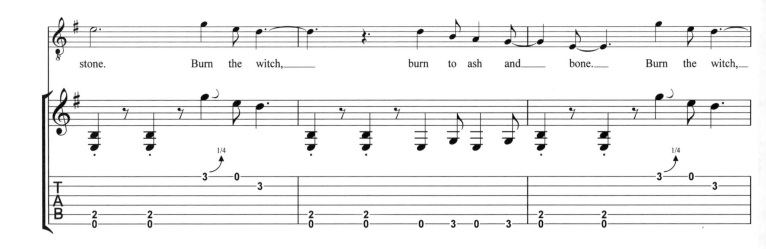

stone. Burn the witch, _____ burn to ash and _____ bone. _____ Burn the witch, _____

_____ burn to ash and _____ bone. Burn the witch, _____ burn to ash and _____

Outro

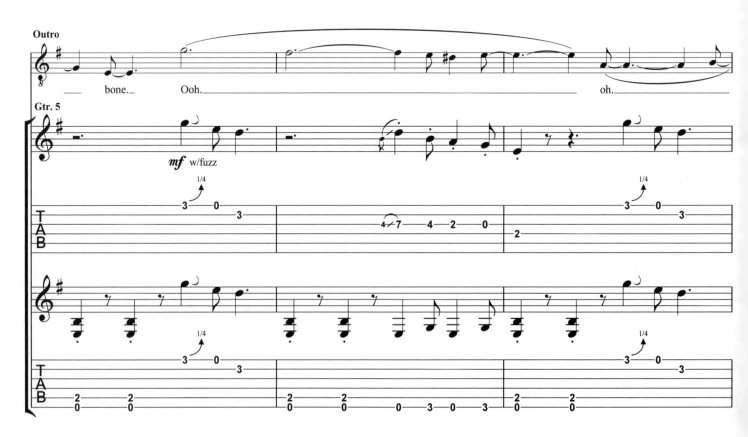

_____ bone. _____ Ooh. _____ oh. _____

Gtr. 5

mf w/fuzz

Ooh,

oh,   oh.

IN MY HEAD

Words & Music by Josh Homme, Alain Johannes, Joey Castillo, Troy Van Leeuwen & Josh Freese

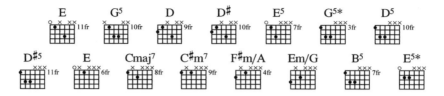

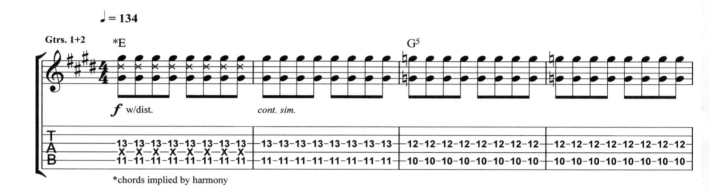

*chords implied by harmony

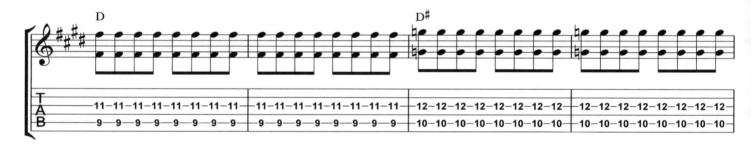

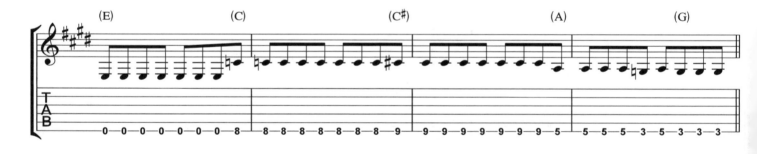

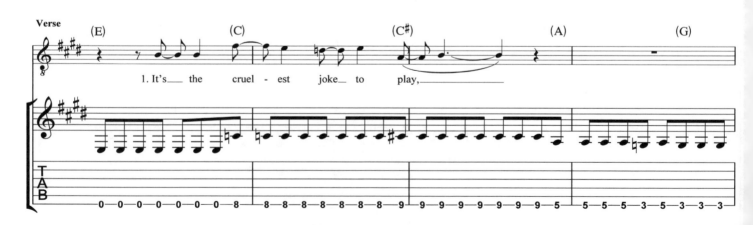

1. It's the cruel-est joke to play,

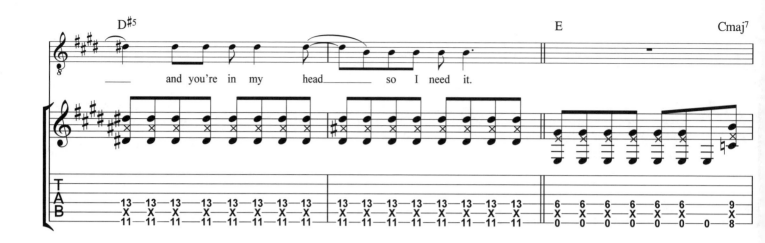

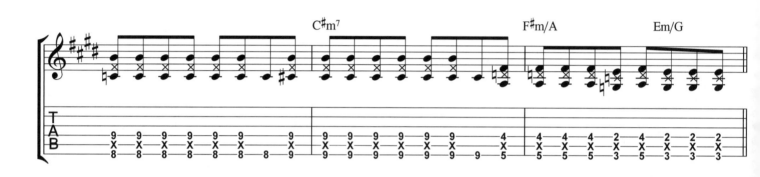

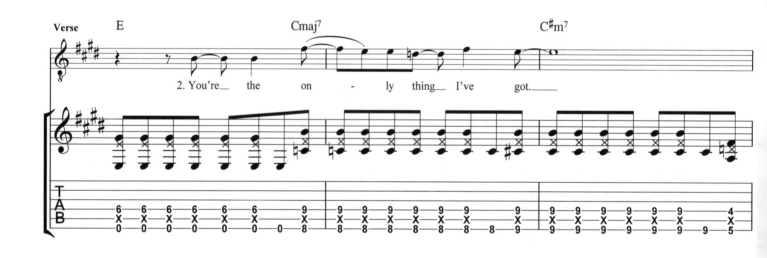

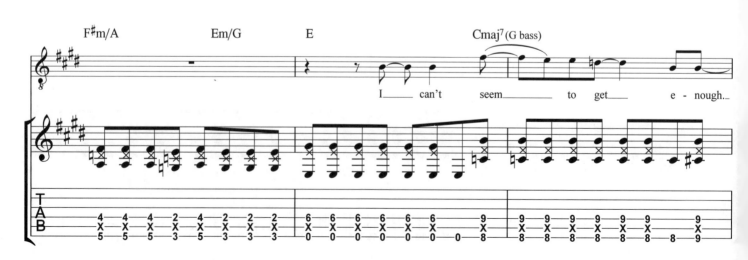

and you're in my head so I need it.
so I need it.

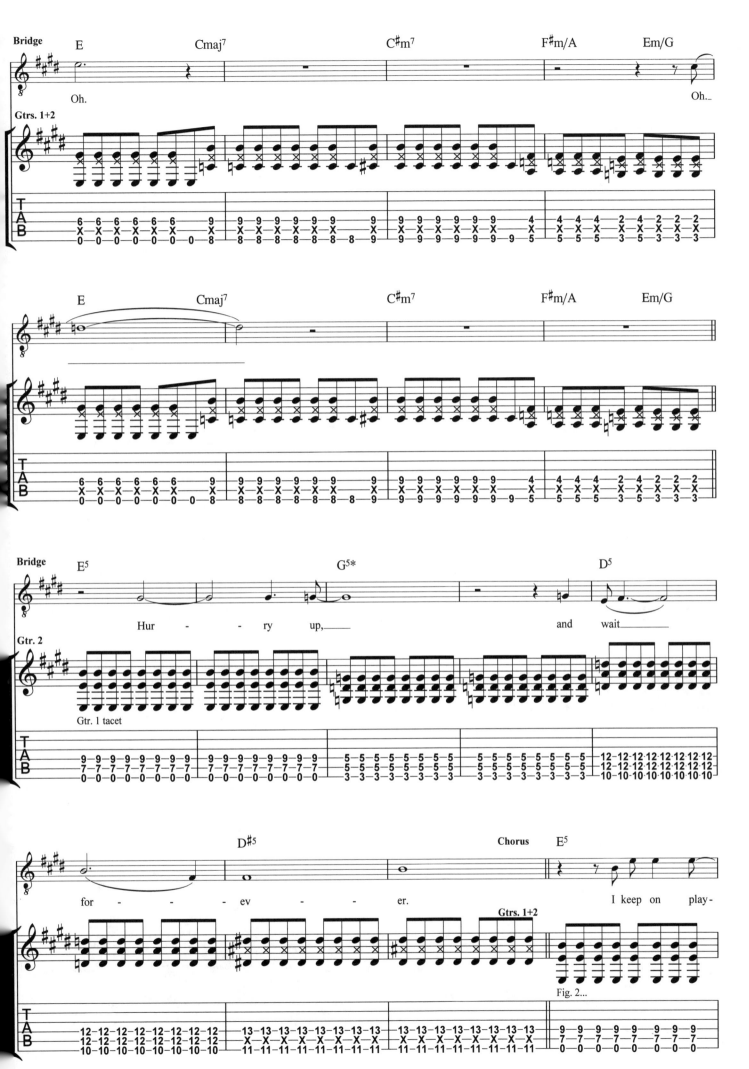

44

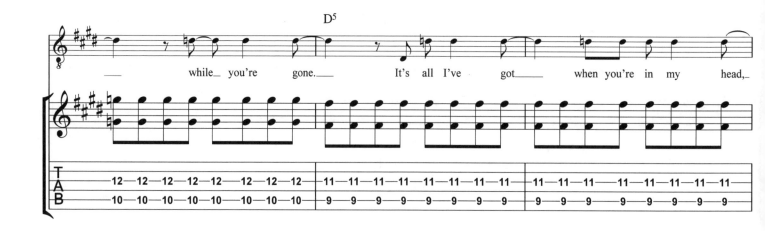

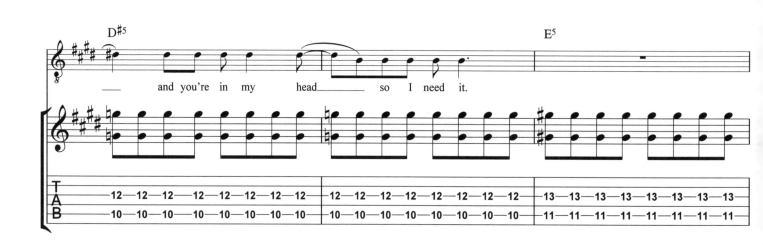

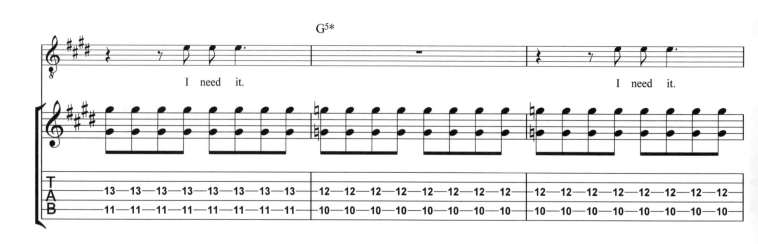

LITTLE SISTER

Words & Music by Josh Homme, Joey Castillo & Troy Van Leeuwen

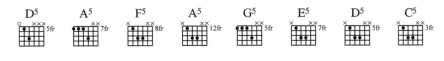

Tune all strings down one semitone. (Original key D♭)

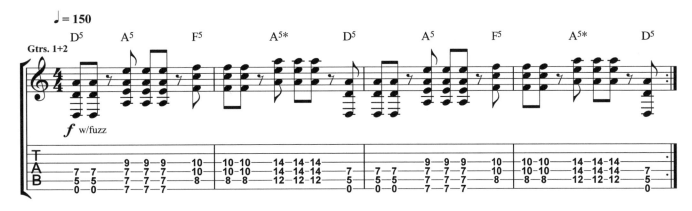

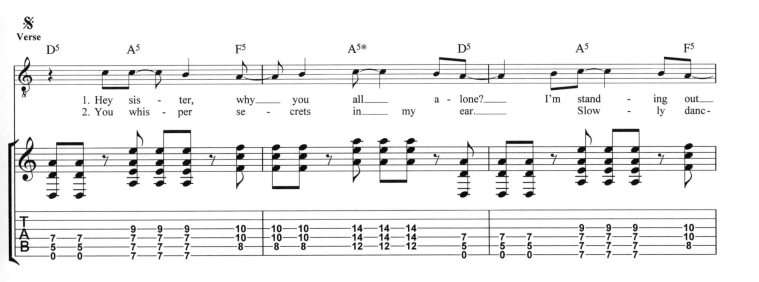

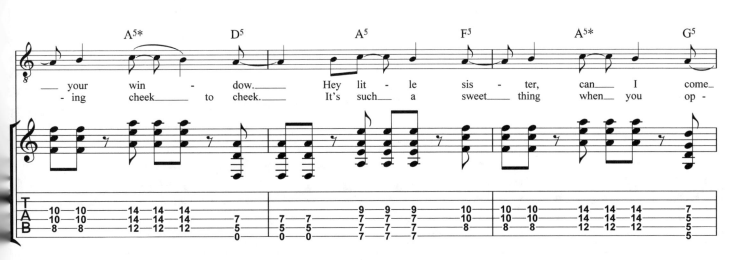

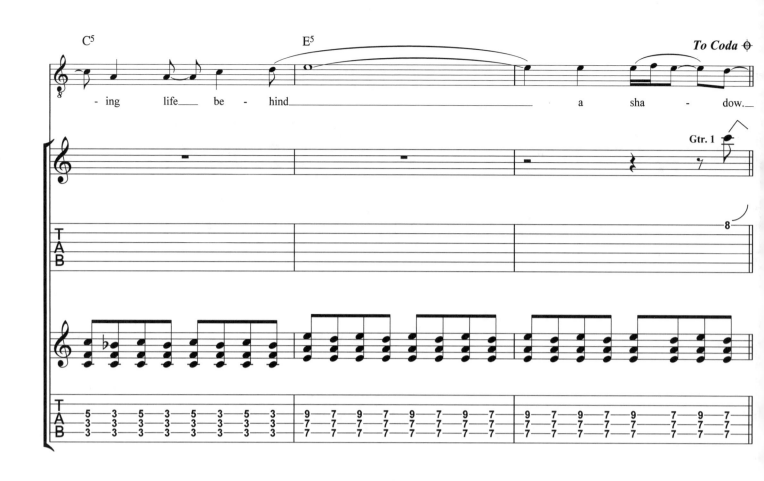

- ing life___ be - hind_____ a sha - dow.___

Interlude

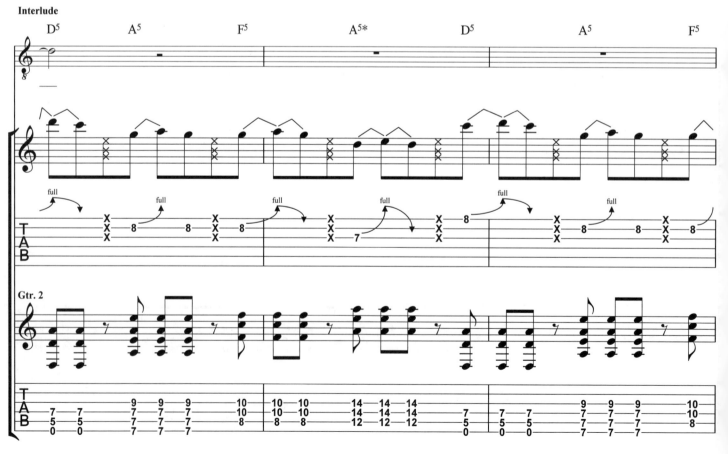

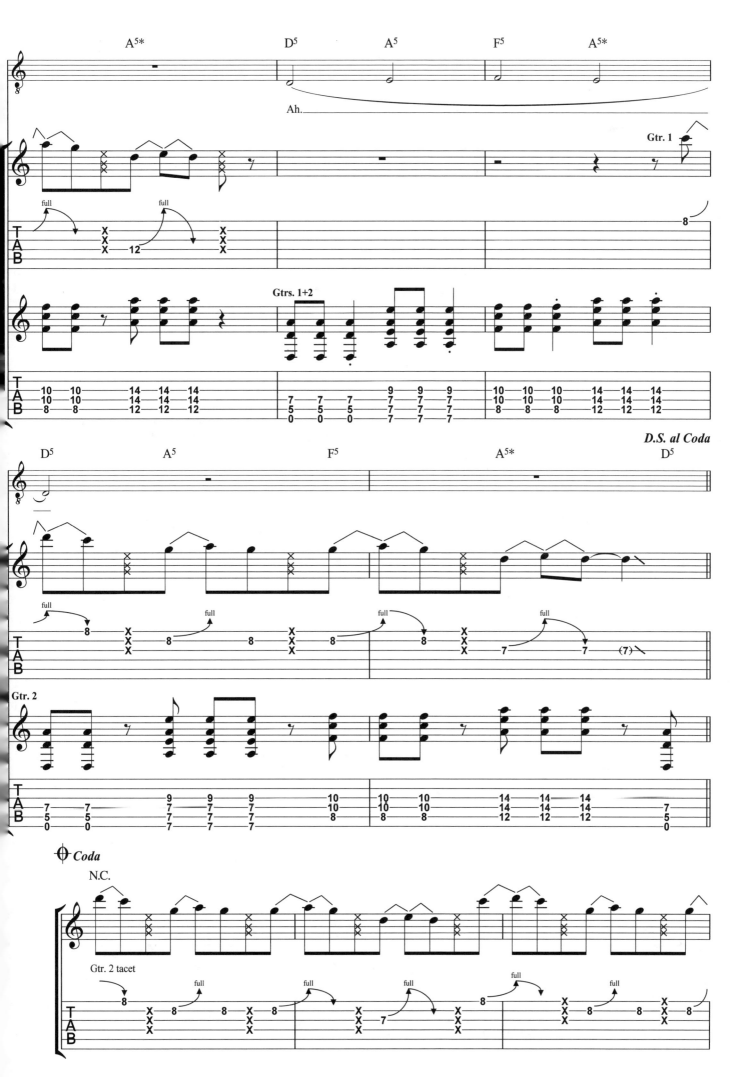

51

*chords implied by harmony

52

53

I NEVER CAME

Words & Music by Josh Homme, Joey Castillo & Troy Van Leeuwen

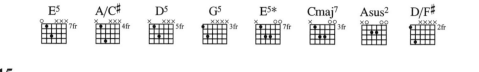

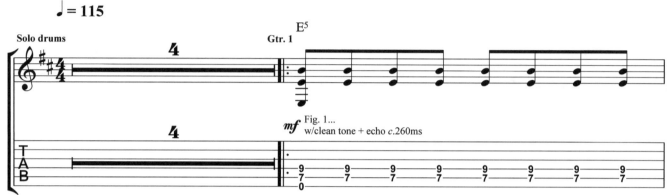

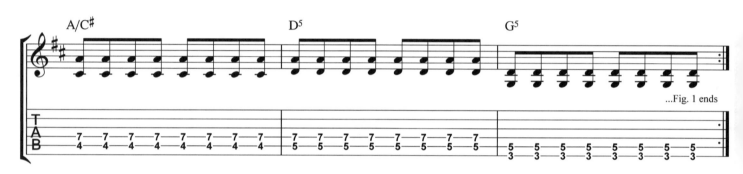

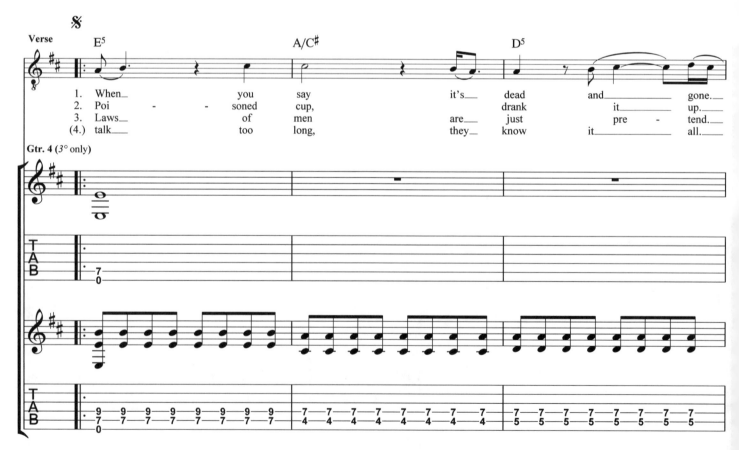

55

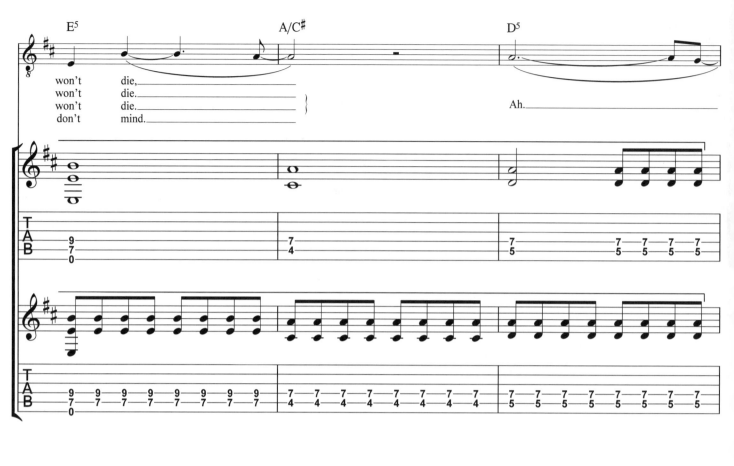

won't die,
won't die.
won't die.
don't mind.

Ah.

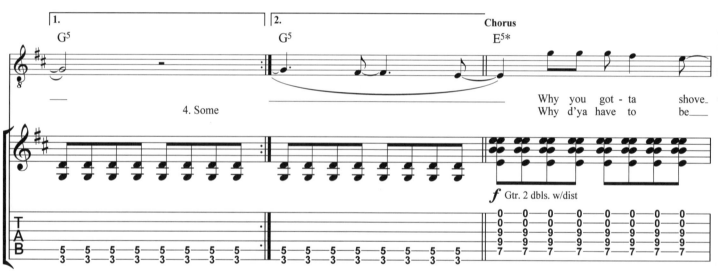

1. G⁵

2. G⁵

Chorus E⁵*

— 4. Some

Why you got-ta shove.
Why d'ya have to be

ff Gtr. 2 dbls. w/dist

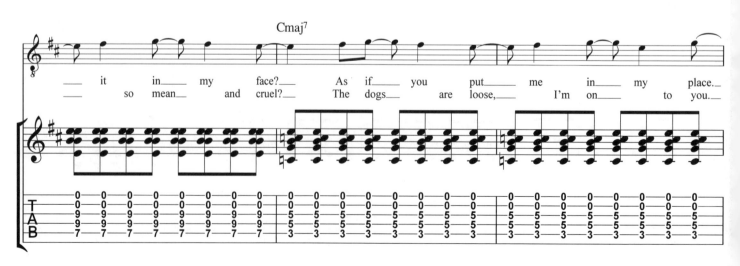

Cmaj⁷

—— it in—— my face? As if—— you put—— me in—— my place.
so mean—— and cruel? The dogs—— are loose, I'm on—— to you.

56

58

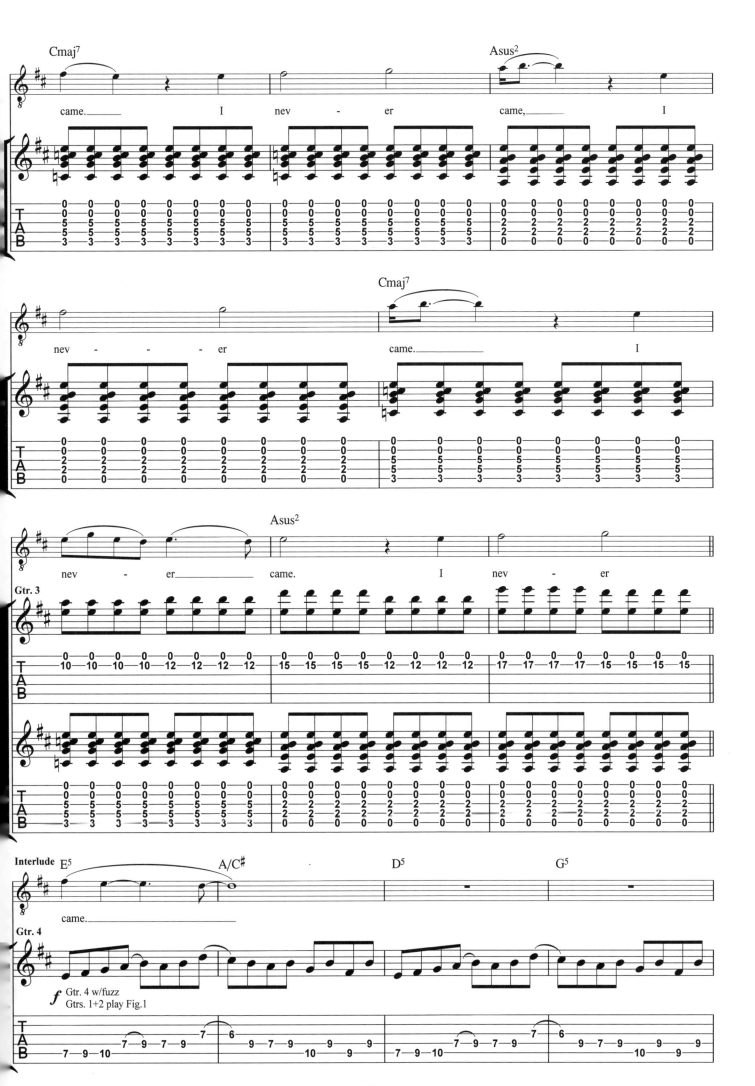

59

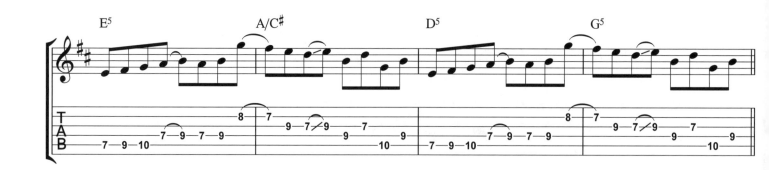

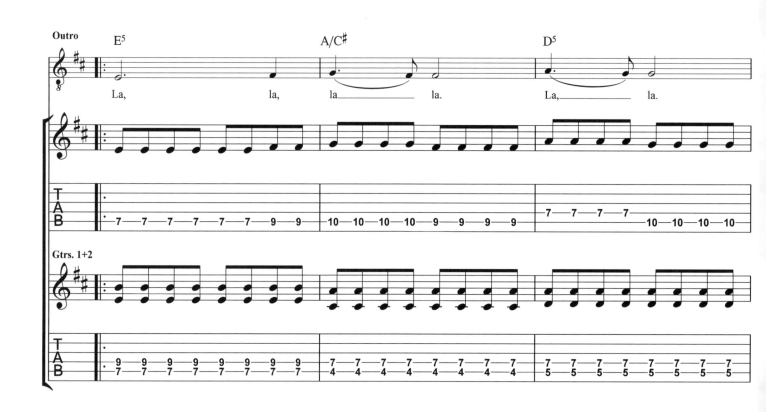

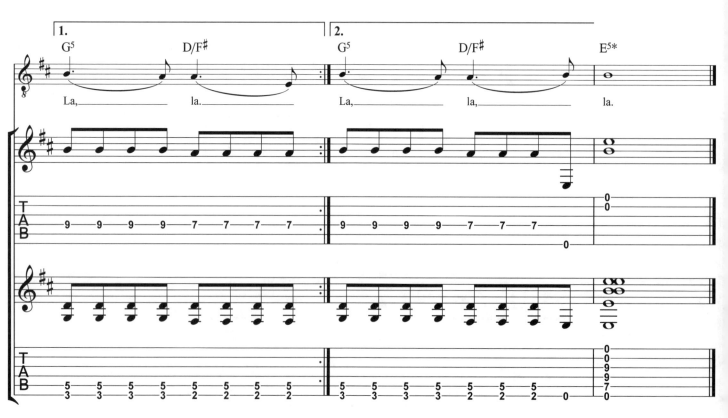

SOMEONE'S IN THE WOLF

Words & Music by Josh Homme, Joey Castillo & Troy Van Leeuwen

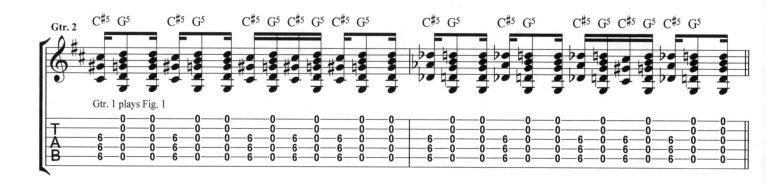

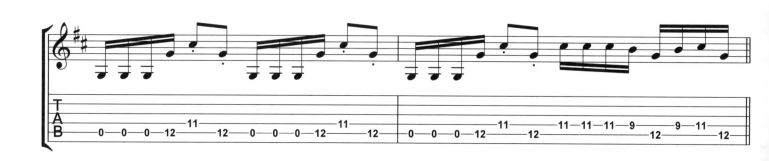

1. Once you're lost in twi-
2. Tempt the fates. Be - ware
(3.) be - tween the trees. A crook-

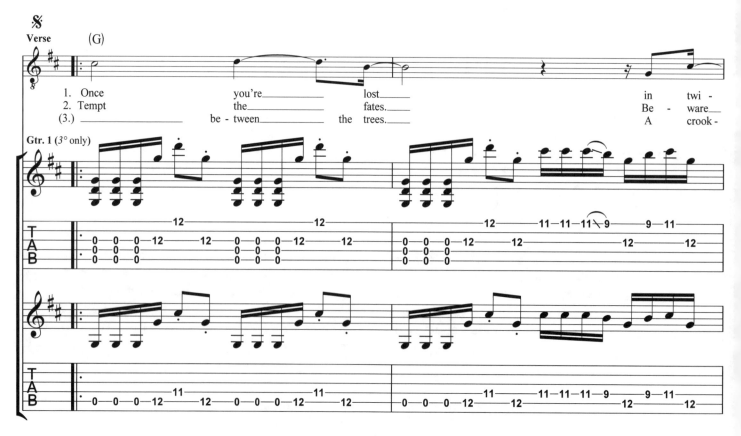

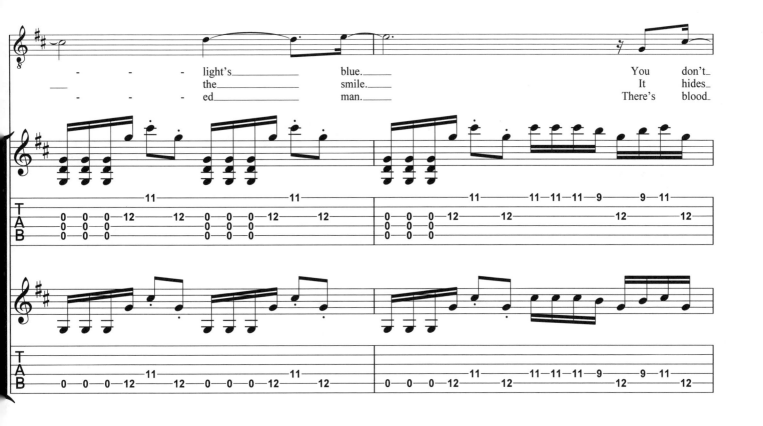

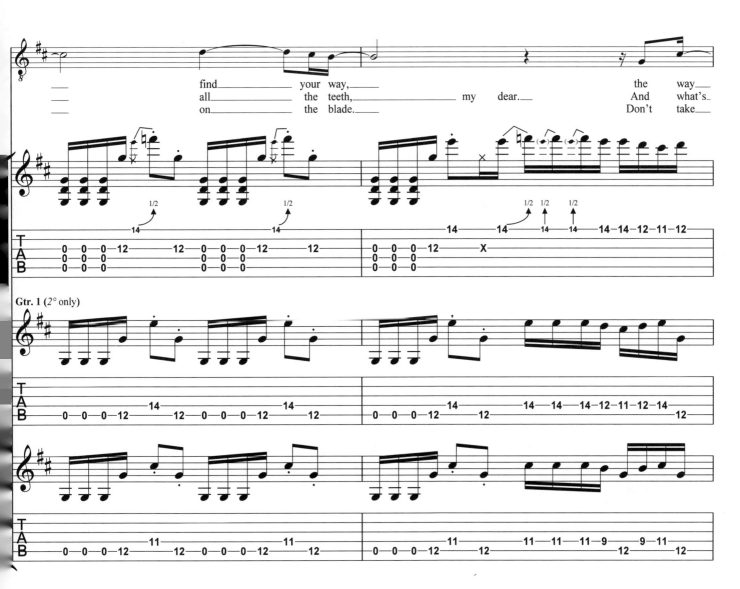

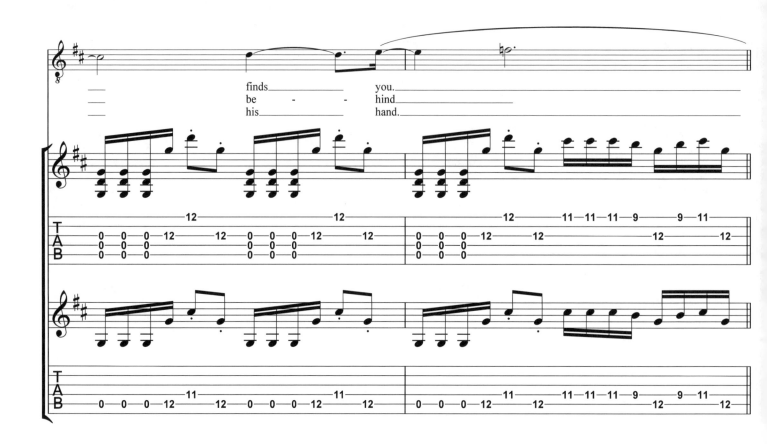

finds_____ you._____
be – – hind_____
his_____ hand._____

them.

Interlude

(G)

Gtrs. 1+2

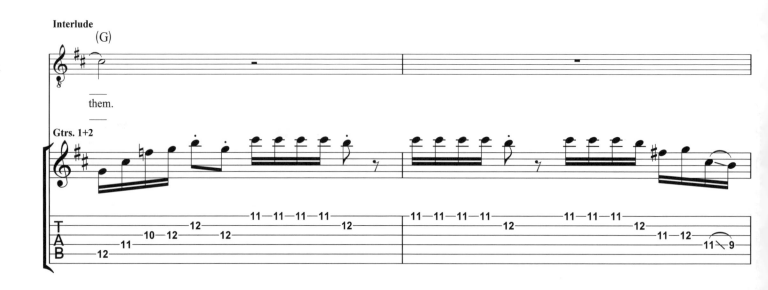

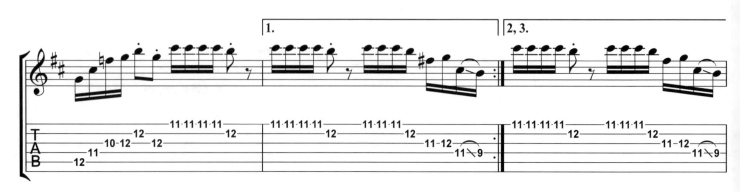

1.

2, 3.

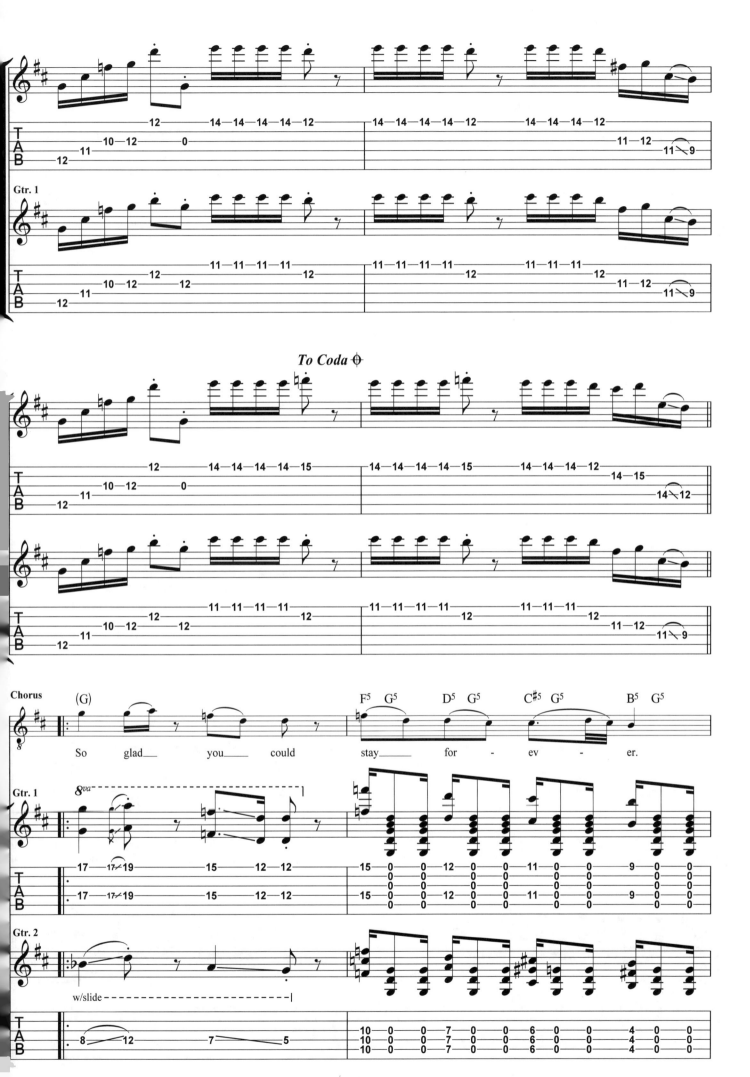

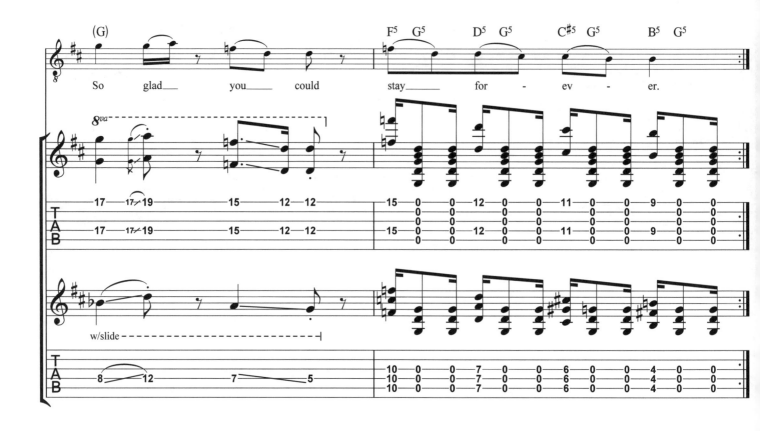

So glad___ you___ could stay___ for - ev - er.

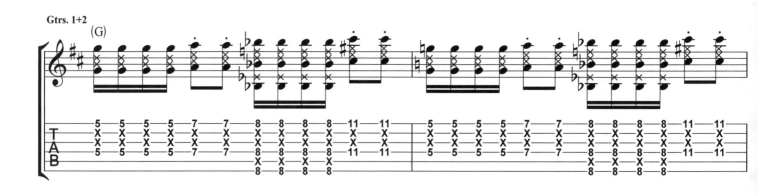

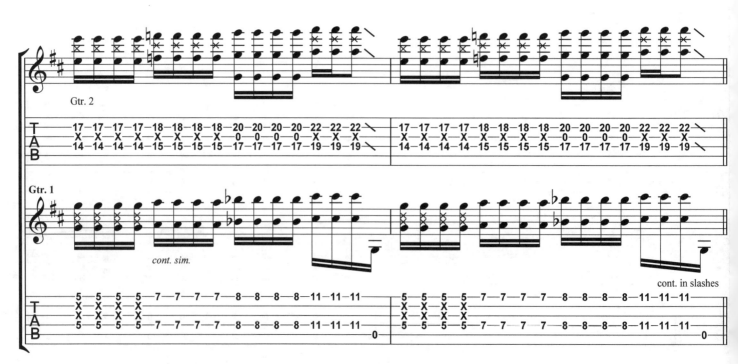

Interlude

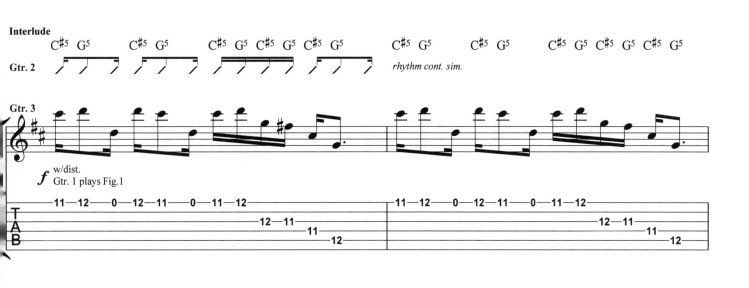

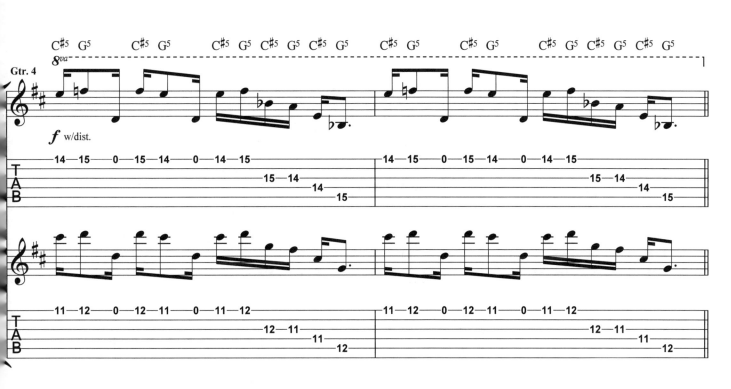

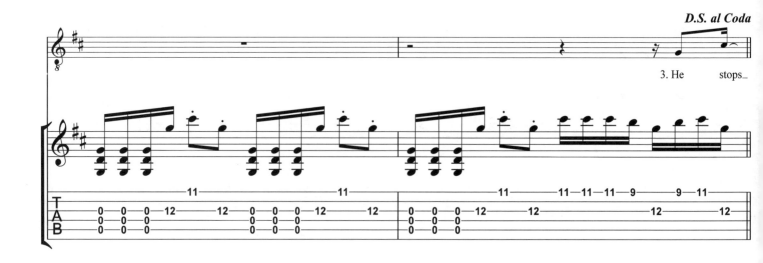

3. He stops___

Coda

4. You warm_____ by_____ the fire-

Gtrs. 1+2

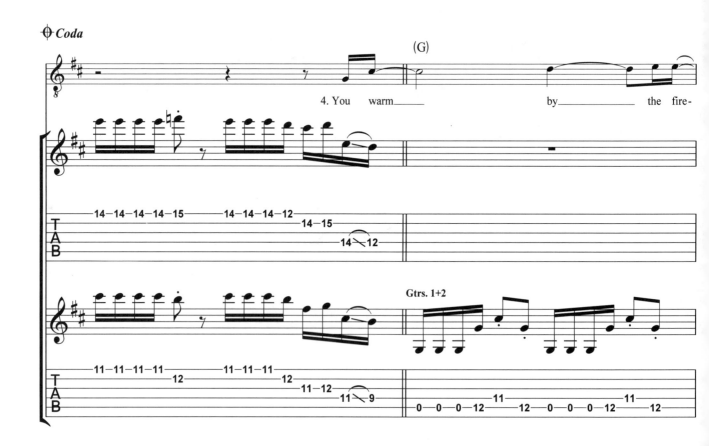

- -light,___ in twi - -light's_____ blue.___

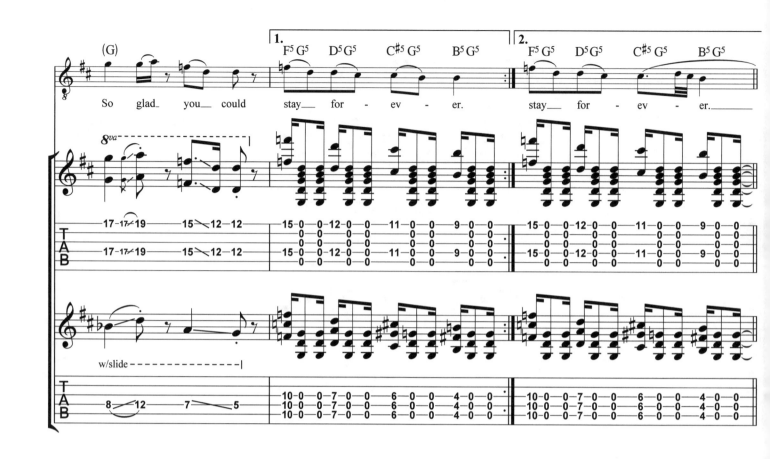

Interlude

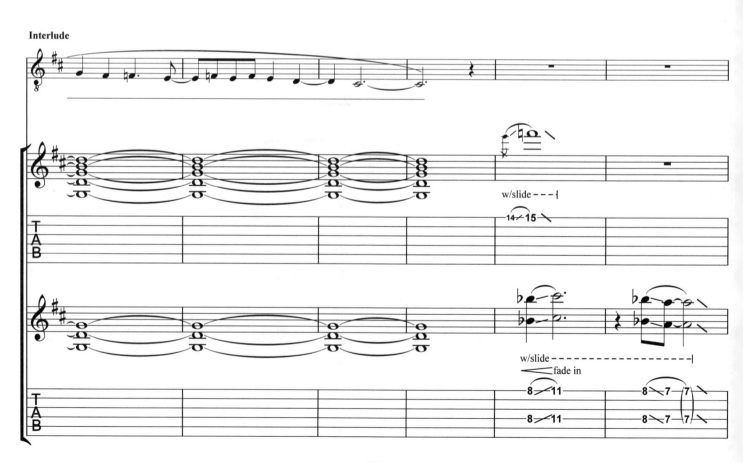

70

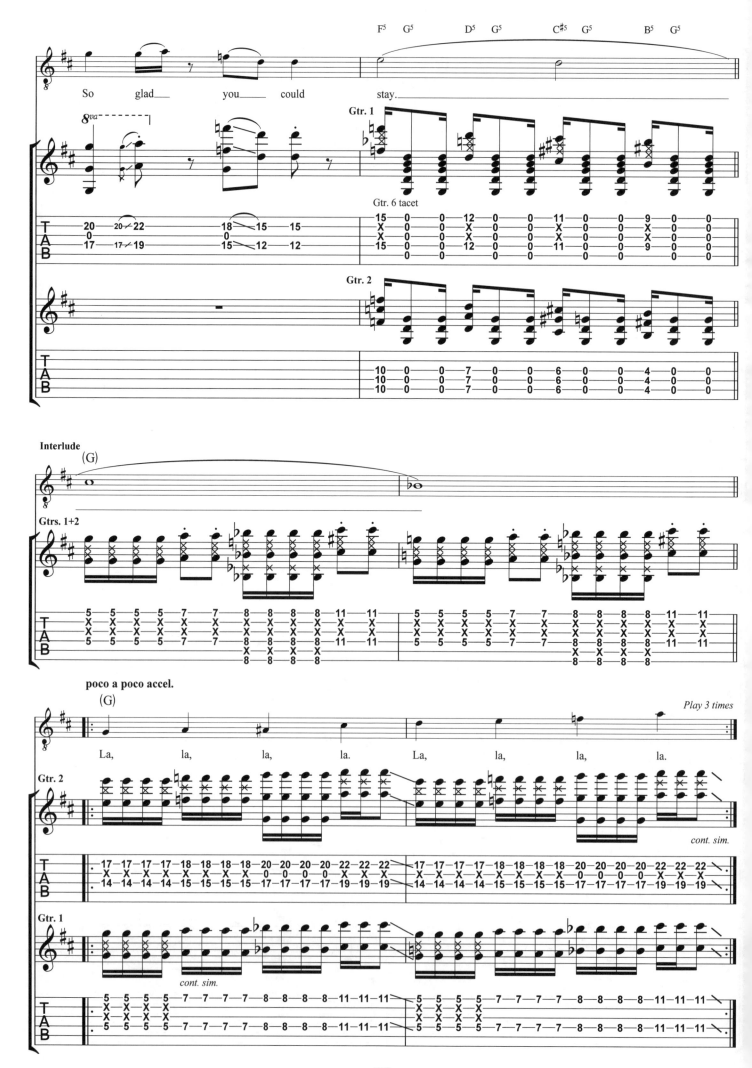

So glad you could stay.

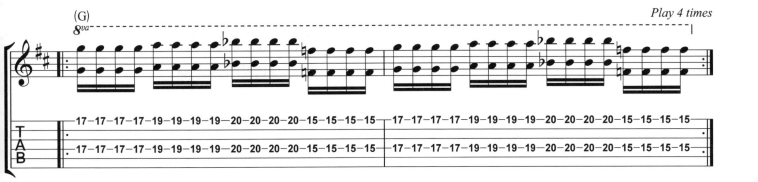

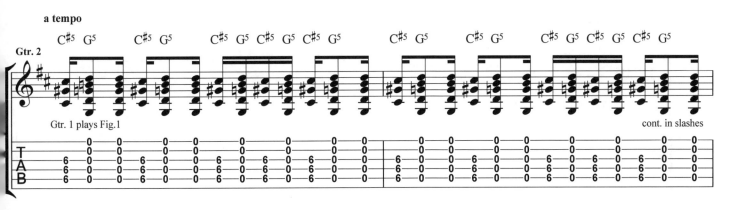

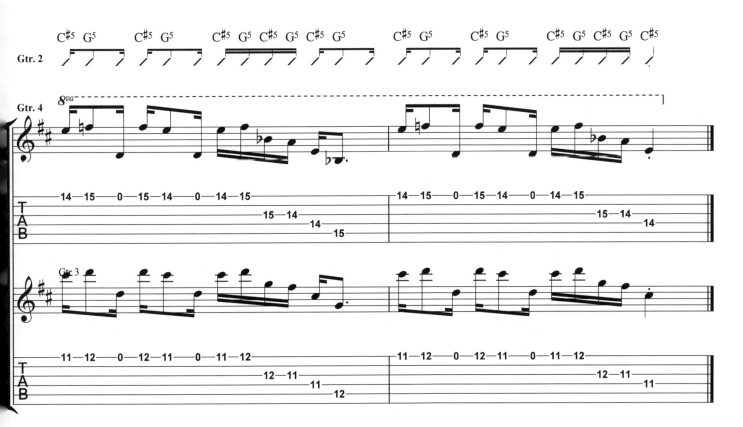

THE BLOOD IS LOVE

Words & Music by Josh Homme, Joey Castillo & Troy Van Leeuwen

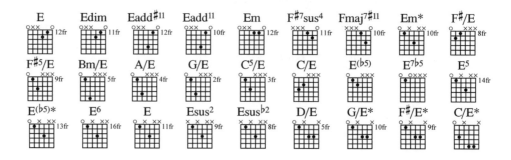

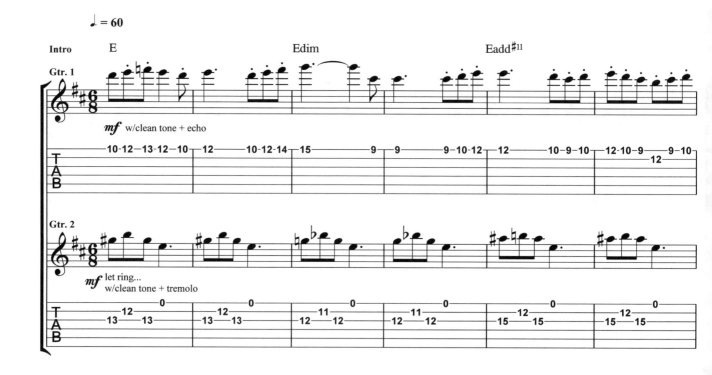

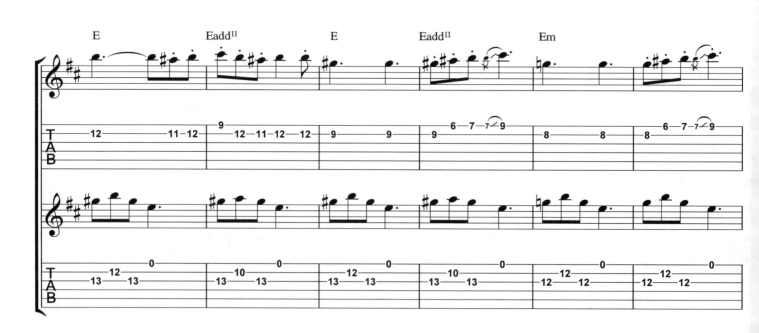

75

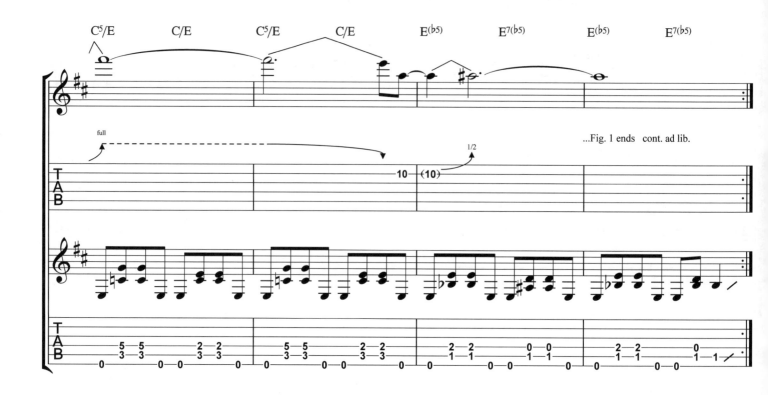

...Fig. 1 ends cont. ad lib.

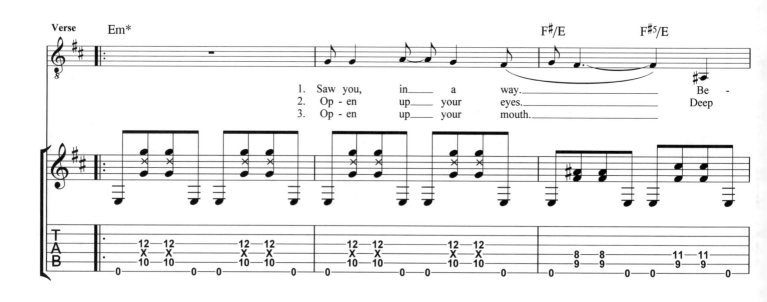

Verse

1. Saw you,   in____ a   way._____   Be -
2. Op - en   up____ your   eyes._____   Deep
3. Op - en   up____ your   mouth._____

-yond   fig - ure____ out____   These   lines_____ of____ life,
blue,   glas - sy____ lake.____   And   swim   'til   wat - er and sky,
Touch   your   lips to____ mine.____   That   we   may   make a____ kiss,

76

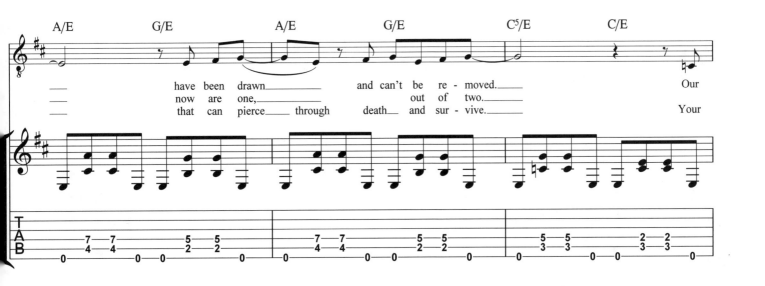

have been drawn_____ and can't be re - moved._____ Our
now are one,_____ out of two._____
that can pierce_____ through death_____ and sur - vive._____ Your

eyes is all it took to_____ know._____
Oh, my blood - shot_____ eyes._____
words have brand - ed_____ my_____ mind._____

Interlude
Gtr. 5

mf w/slight dist.

let ring...

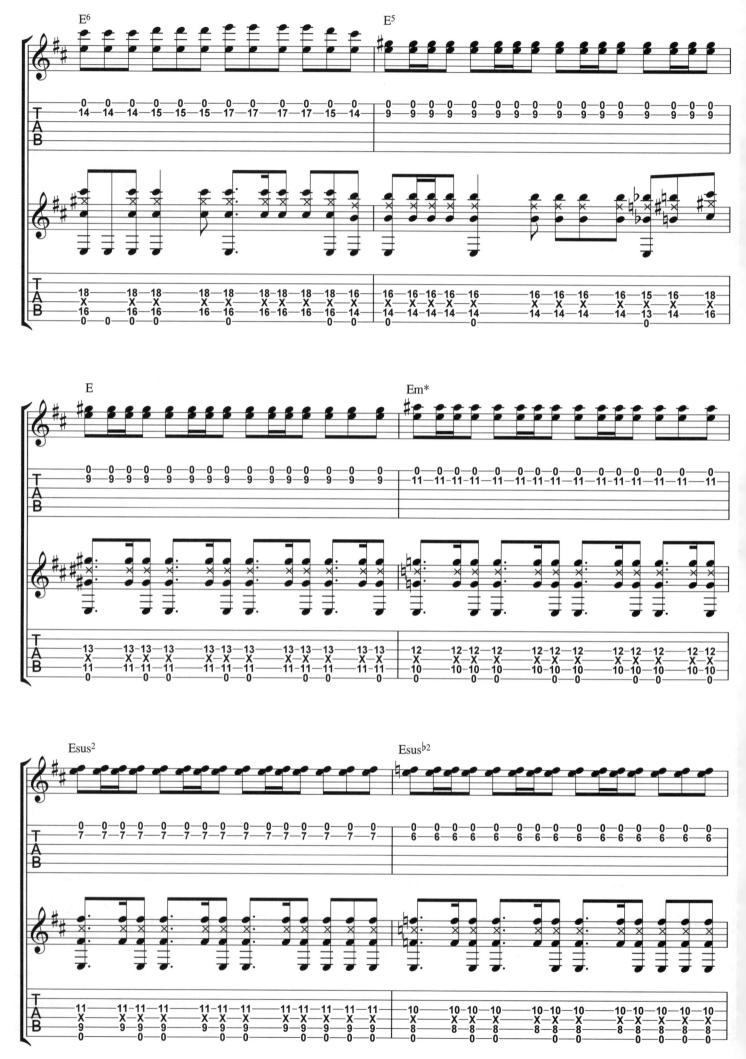

79

SKIN ON SKIN

Words & Music by Josh Homme, Joey Castillo & Troy Van Leeuwen

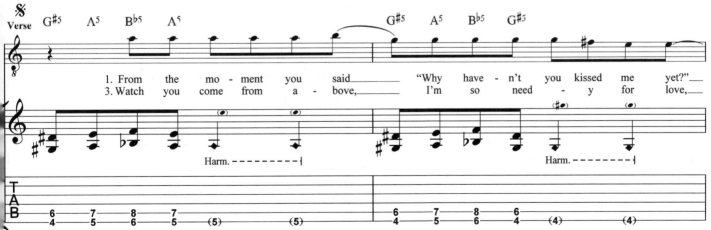

but I love to watch you go,_____ ba - by. Twist - ed sec - ret lives,_____

the way you bat your_____ eyes,_____ giv - ing head,_____ giv - ing head._____ Oh, yeah!_____

Gtr. Solo

Gtr. 2

f w/dist.+wah-wah

Fig. 1 - |

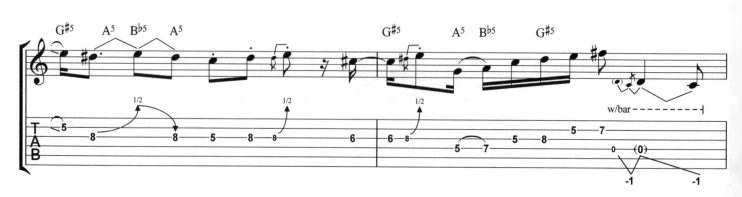

w/bar - - - - - - - - - |

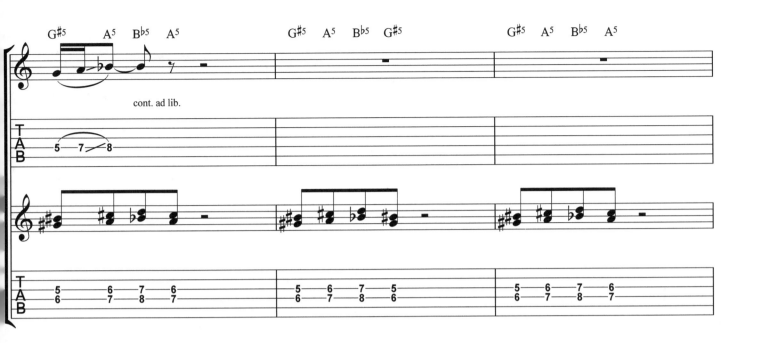

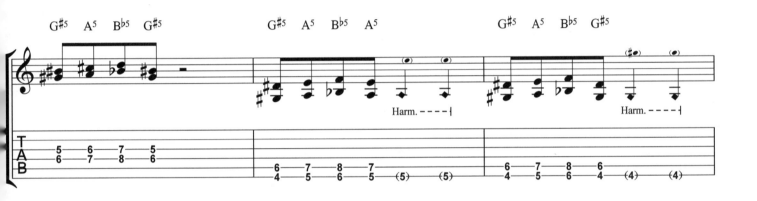

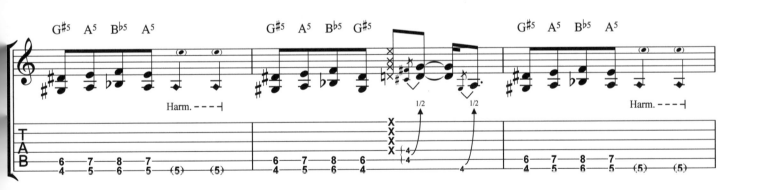

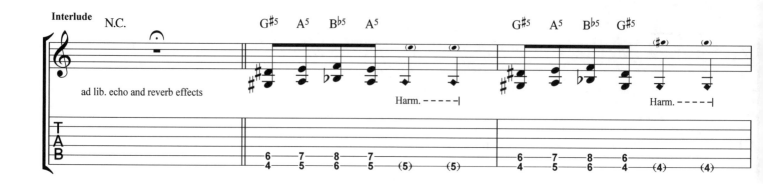

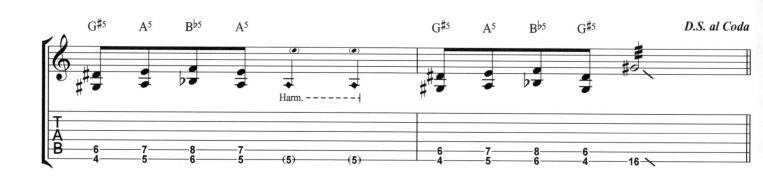

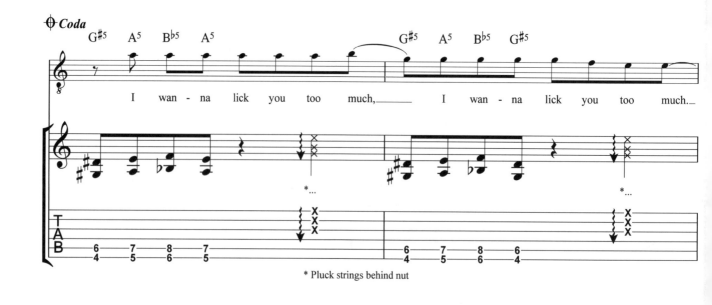

* Pluck strings behind nut

BROKEN BOX

Words & Music by Josh Homme, Joey Castillo & Troy Van Leeuwen

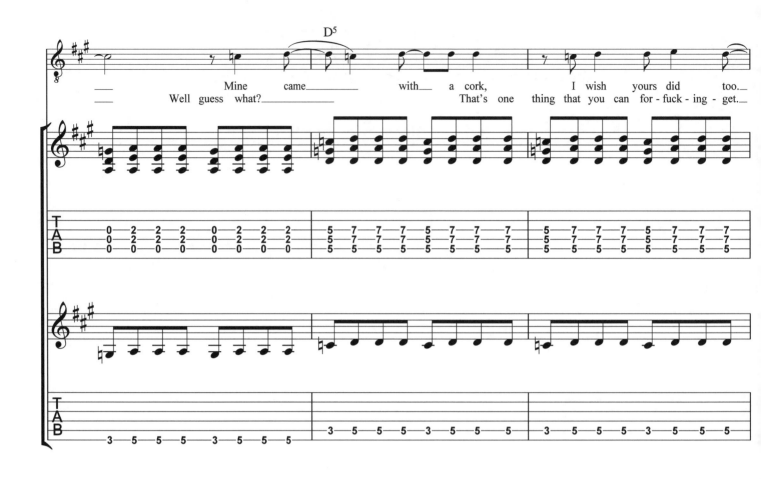

Mine came_____ with a cork, I wish yours did too._____
Well guess what?_____ That's one thing that you can for - fuck - ing - get._____

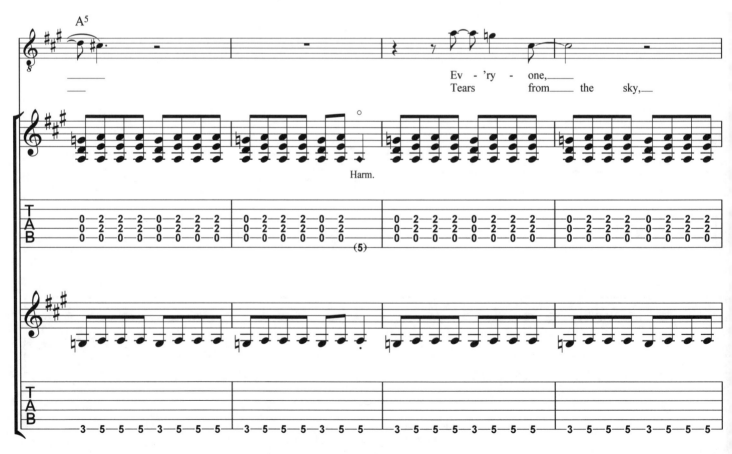

Ev - 'ry - one,_____
Tears from_____ the sky,_____

Harm.

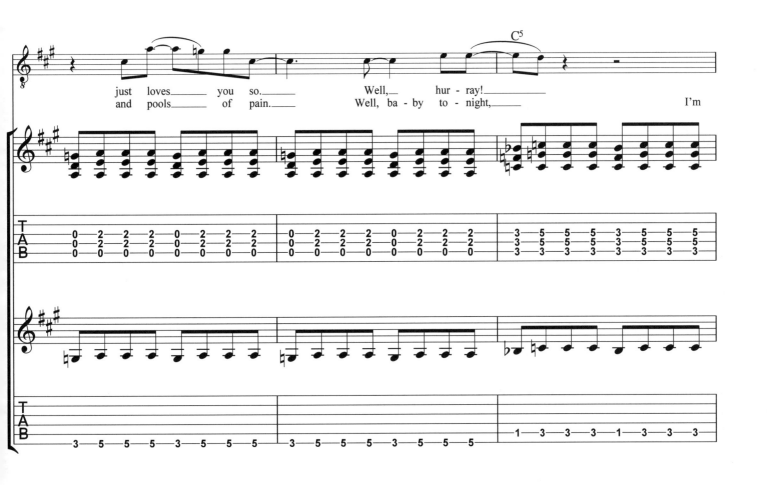

just loves you so.
and pools of pain. Well, baby to - night,
Well, hur - ray!
I'm

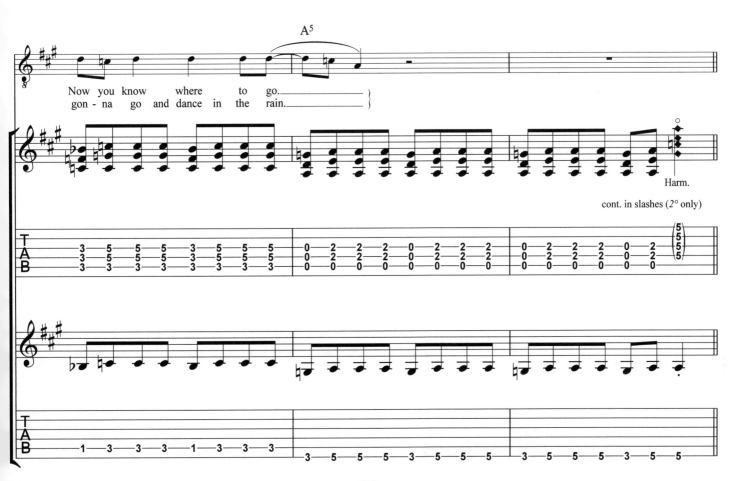

Now you know where to go.
gon - na go and dance in the rain.

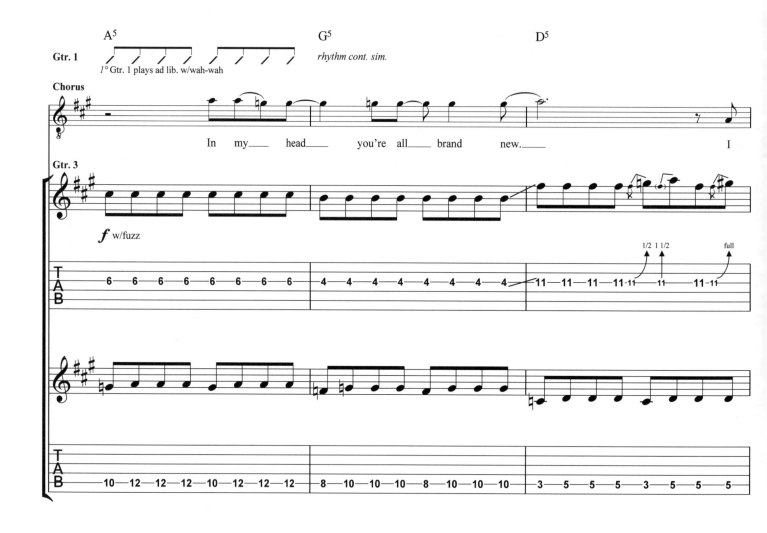

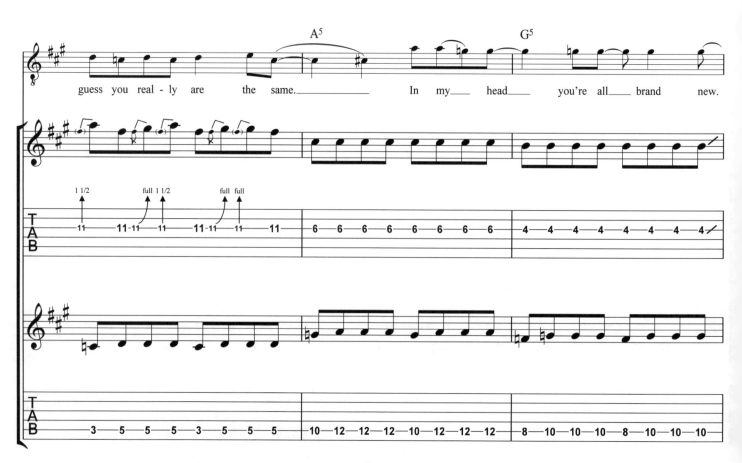

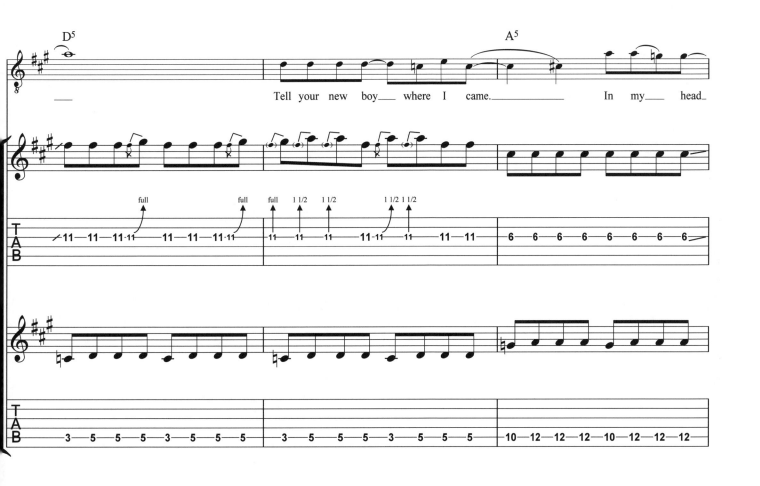

Tell your new boy___ where I came.___ In my___ head___

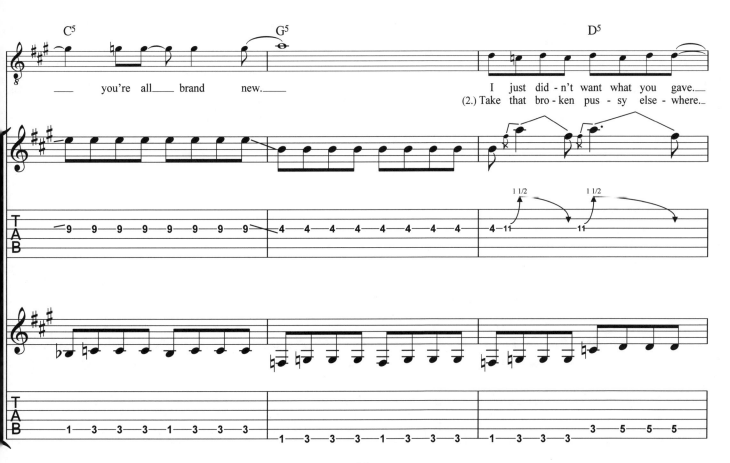

___ you're all___ brand new.___

I just did-n't want what you gave.___
(2.) Take that bro-ken pus-sy else-where.___

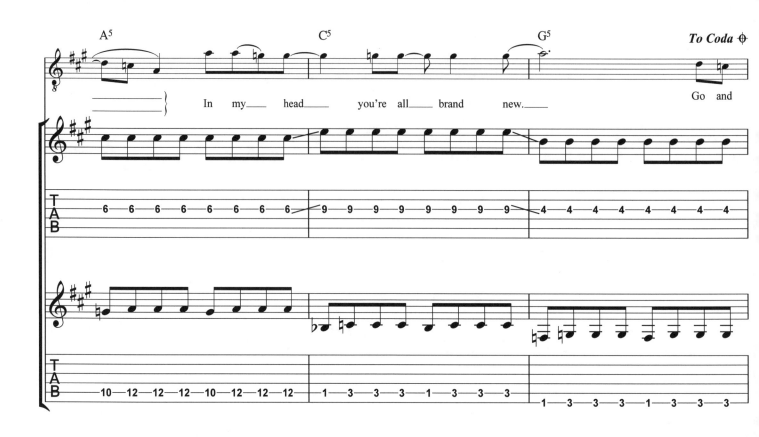

In my___ head___ you're all___ brand new.___ Go and

find your-self an-oth - er slave._____ Doo-

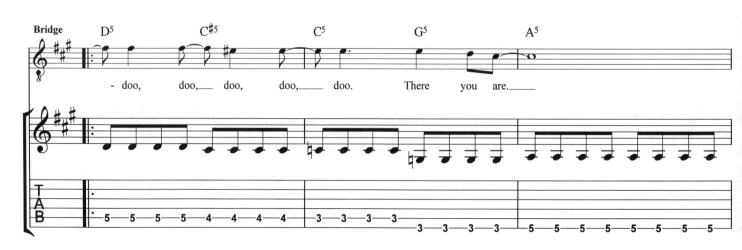

Bridge

- doo, doo,___ doo, doo,___ doo. There you are.___

95

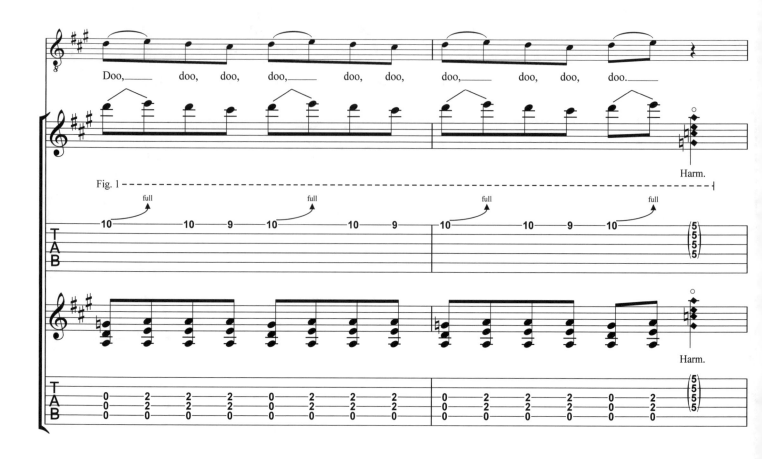

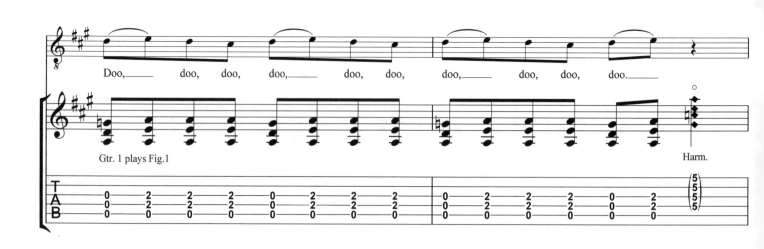

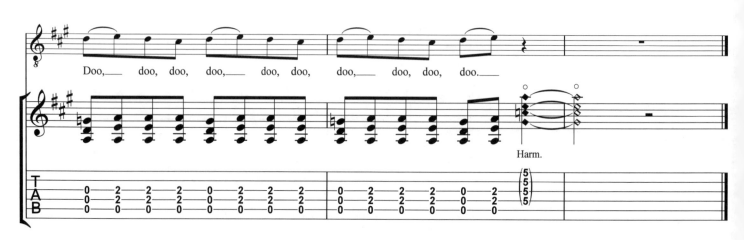

"YOU GOT A KILLER SCENE THERE, MAN..."

Words & Music by Josh Homme, Joey Castillo & Troy Van Leeuwen

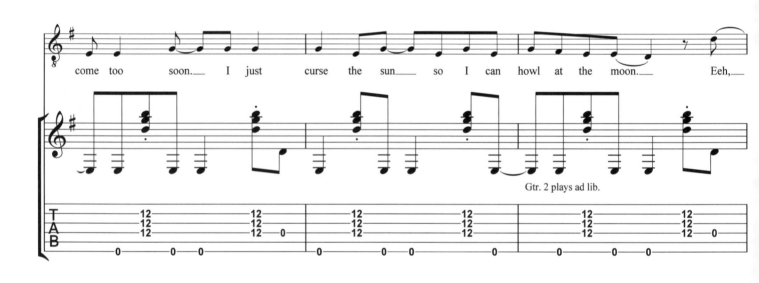

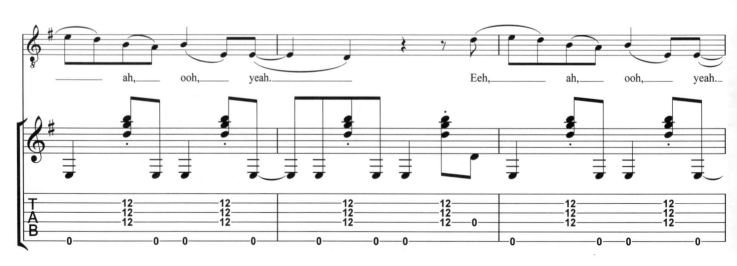

2. Don't wan - na

Verse Em⁷

love you no more,_ don't wan - na love you_ less._ I wan - na be crushed_ by your sweet_
- u - ni - ted, by drift - ing a - lone. This is the ar - my of none,_ got no flag,_

cont. ad lib.

2° ad lib.

101

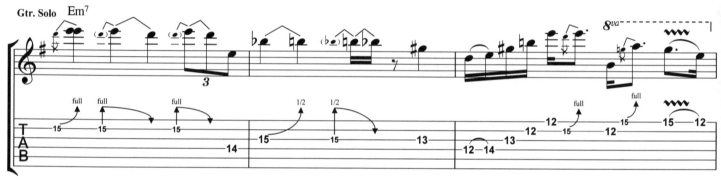

Gtr. Solo Em⁷

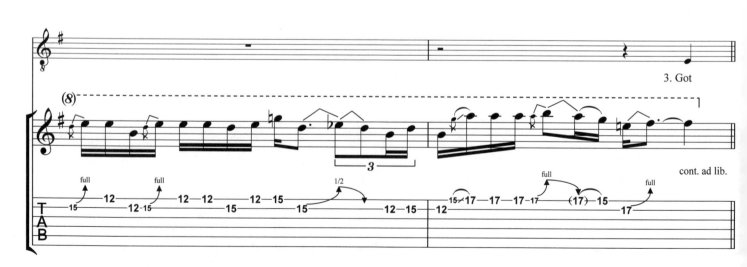

3. Got

cont. ad lib.

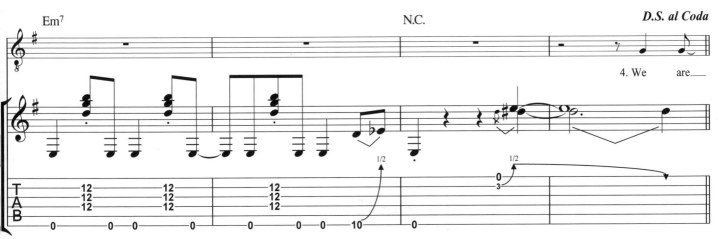

LONG SLOW GOODBYE

Words & Music by Josh Homme, Mark Lanegan, Joey Castillo & Troy Van Leeuwen

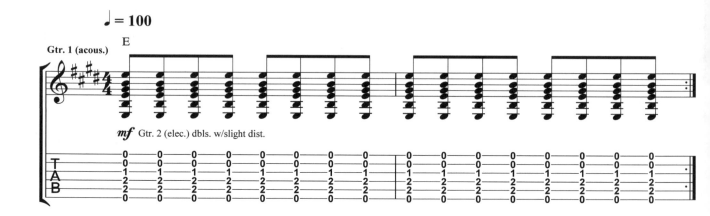

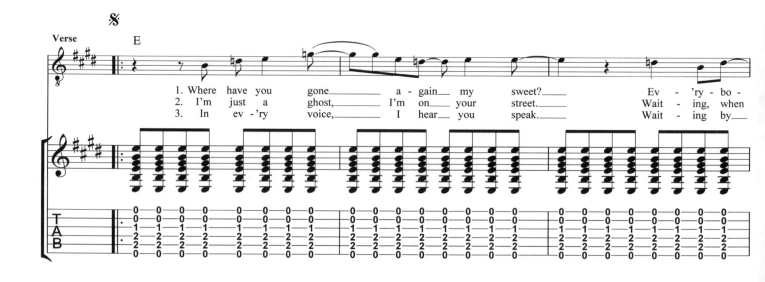

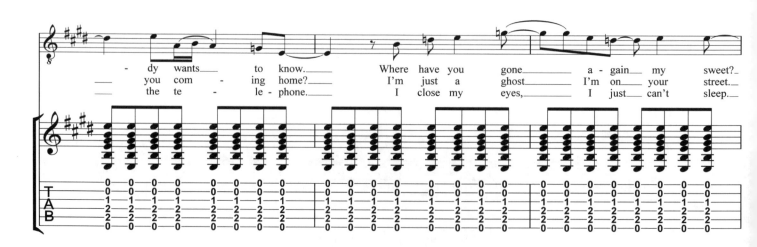

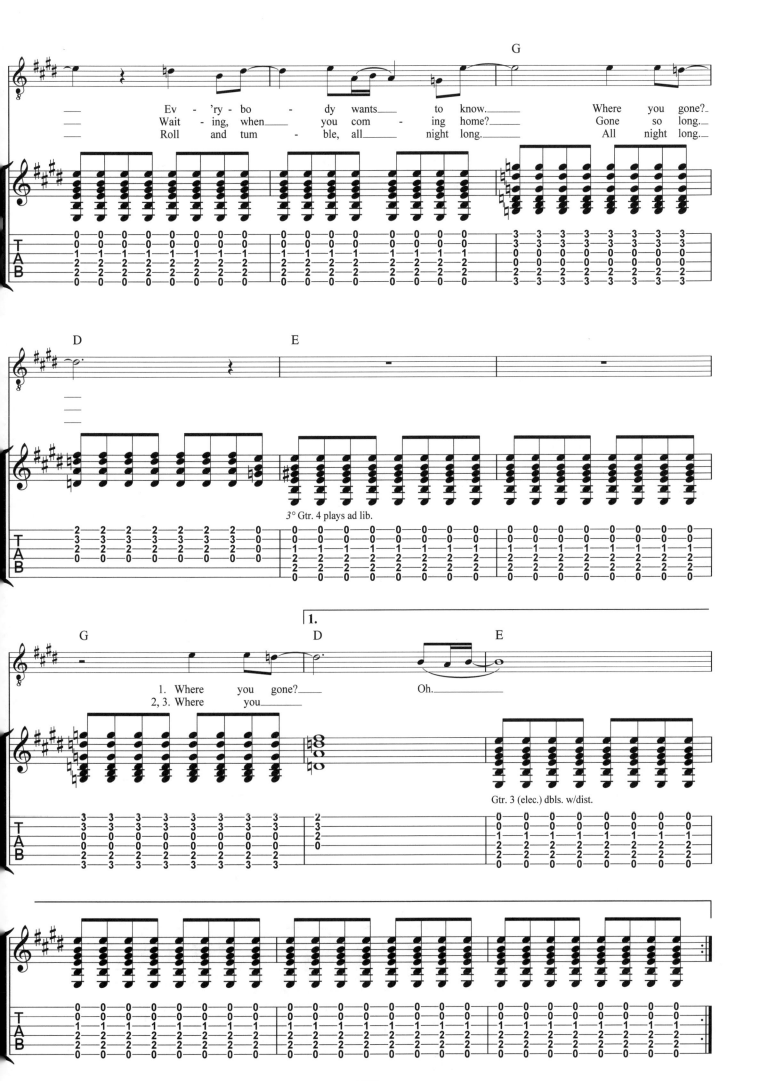

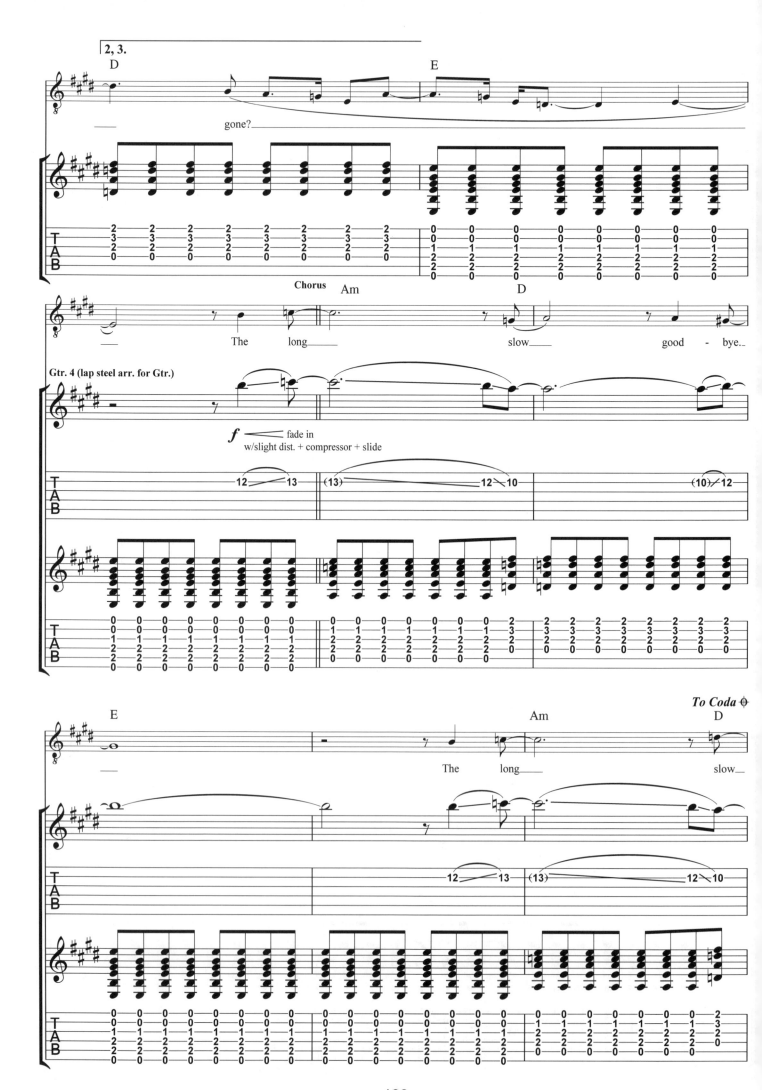

good - bye.

D.S. al Coda

Coda

good - bye.

The long

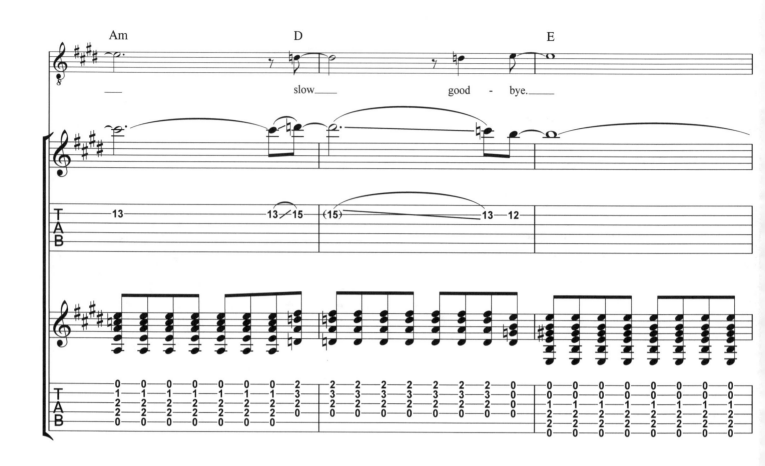

slow_____ good - bye.

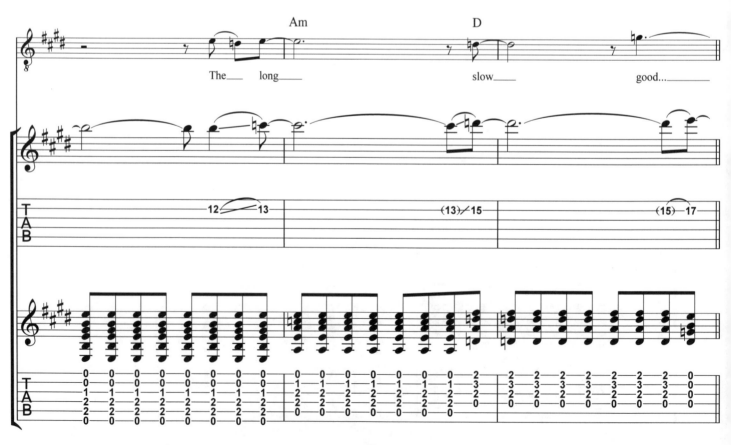

The_____ long_____ slow_____ good...____

Interlude

Gtr. 1
(acous.)

Gtr. 2 plays ad lib.

Gtr. 1 tacet

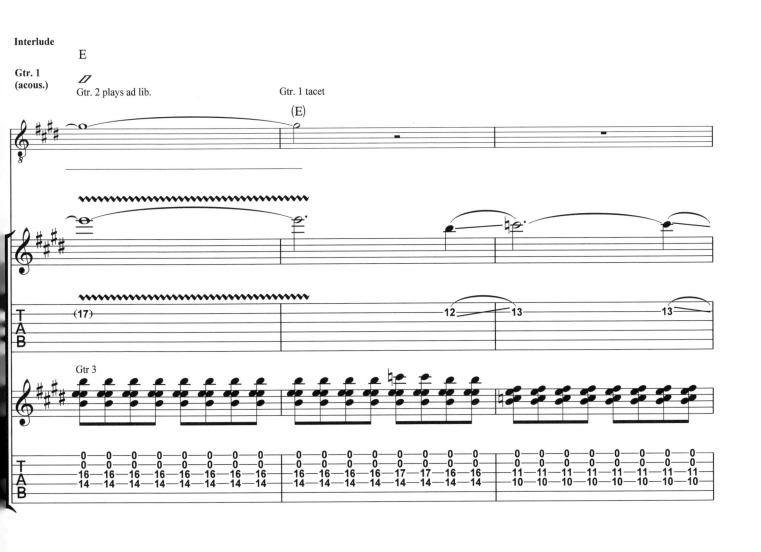

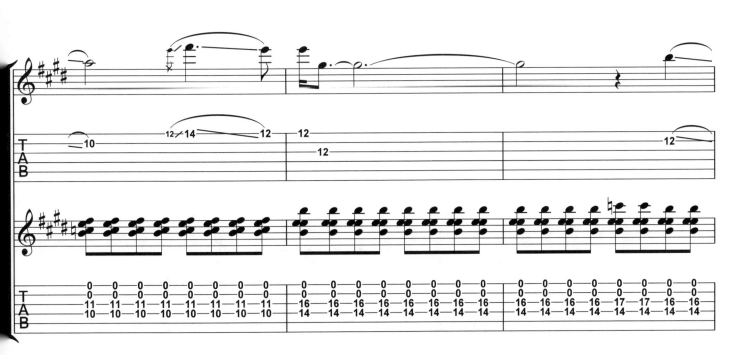

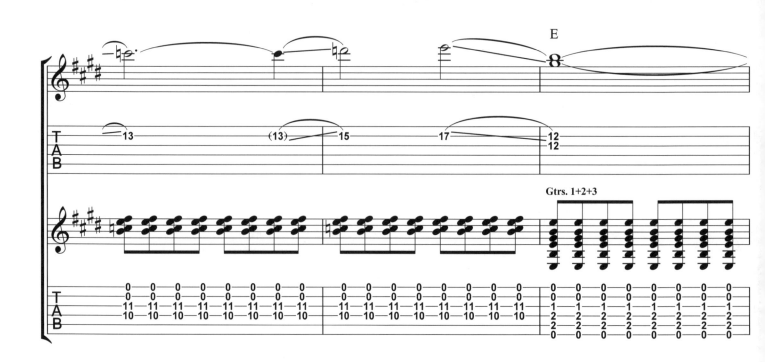

Gtr. 4 tacet

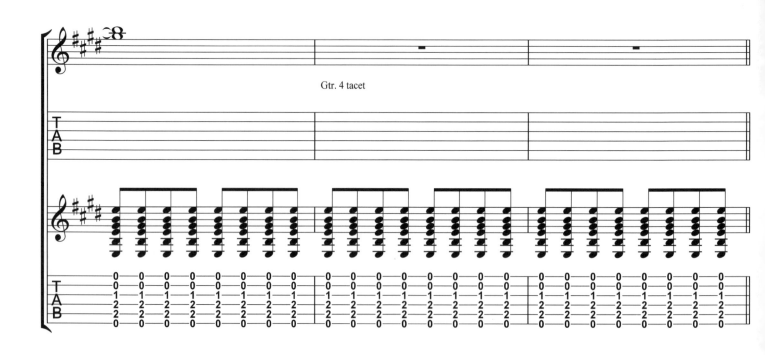

Verse

4. I close my eyes,____ I just____ can't____ sleep.____

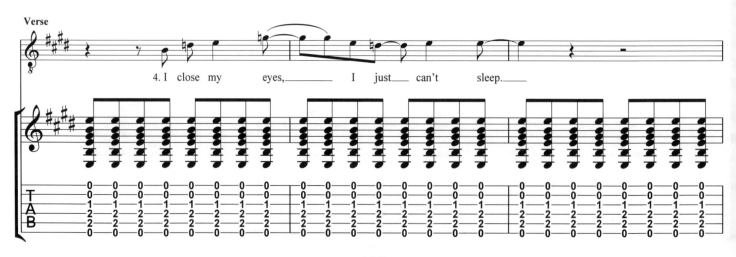

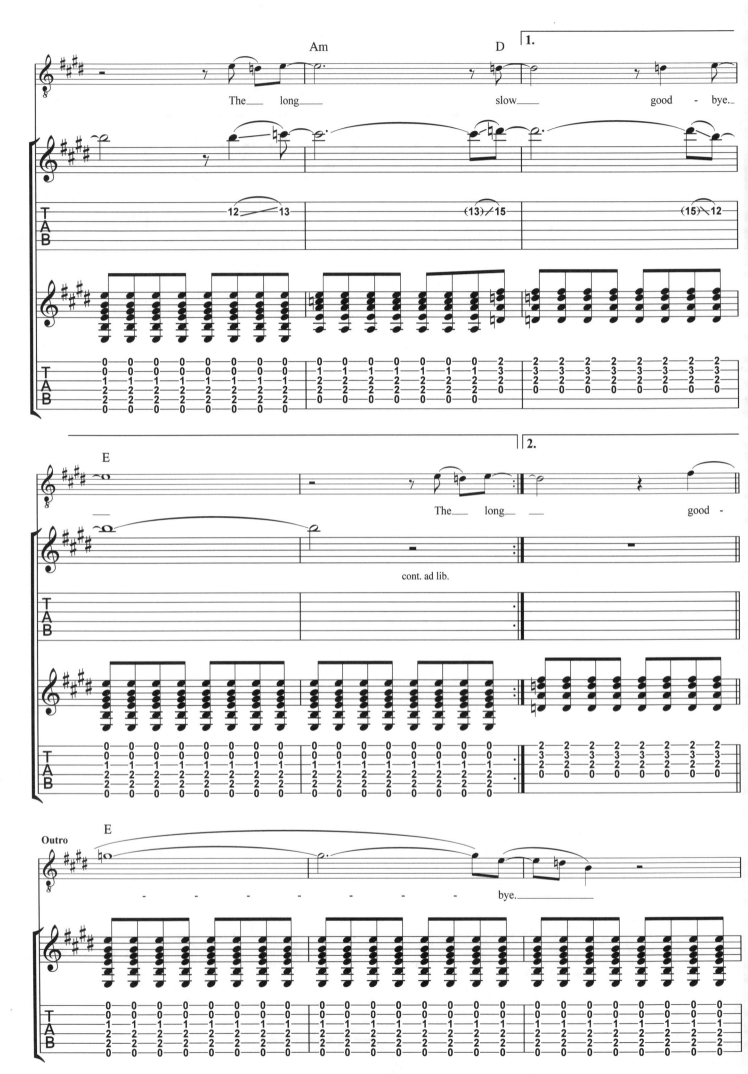

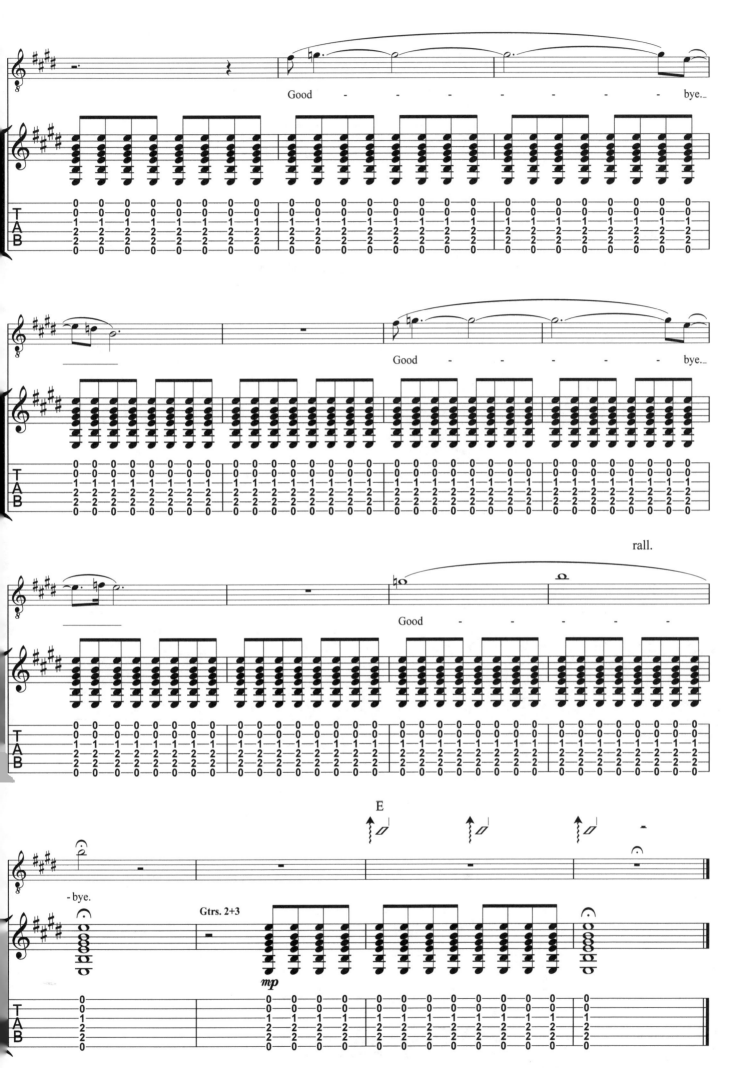

LIKE A DRUG

Words & Music by Josh Homme, Joey Castillo & Troy Van Leeuwen

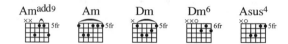

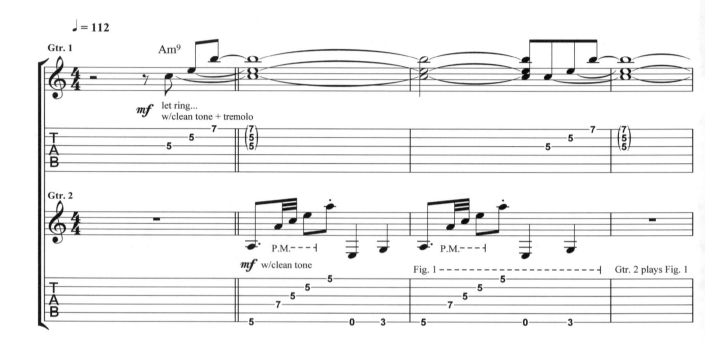

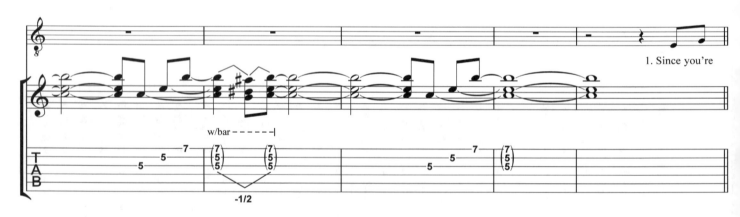

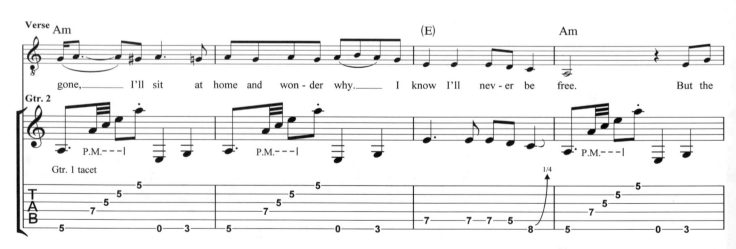

117

120

PRECIOUS AND GRACE

Words & Music by Billy Gibbons, Dusty Hill & Frank Beard

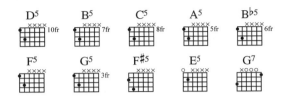

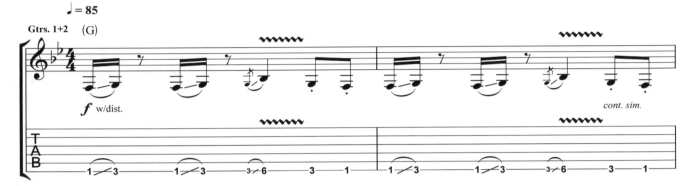

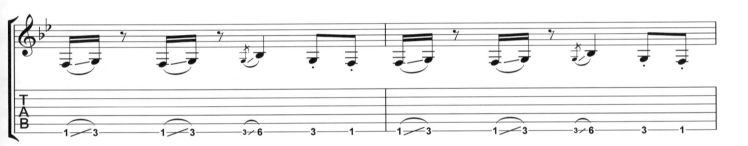

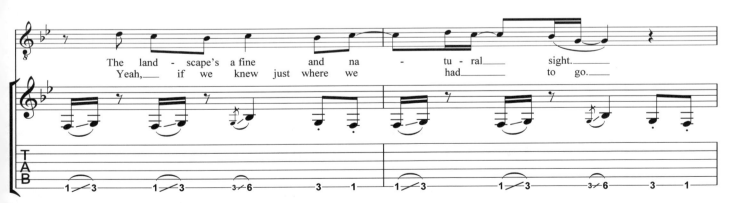

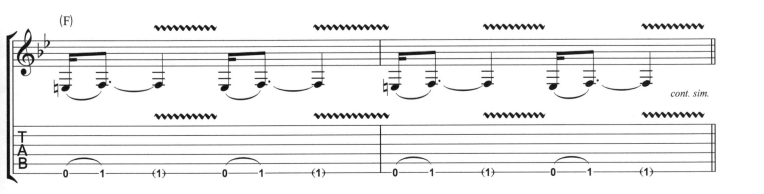

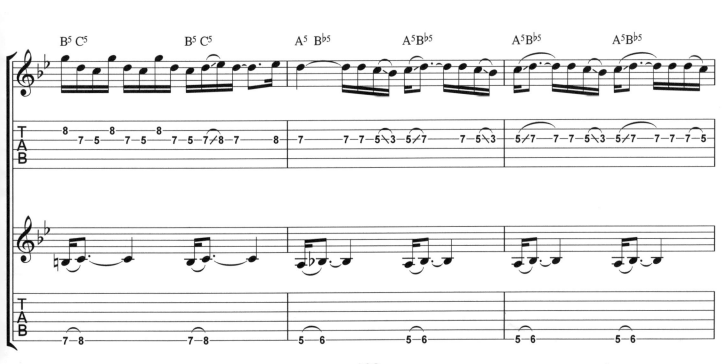

Verse

3. So if you're out rid-ing late one night._____ Man,__ you see that su-per-na-tur-al de-light.__

Gtr. 3 tacet
Gtr. 2 plays Fig. 1

124

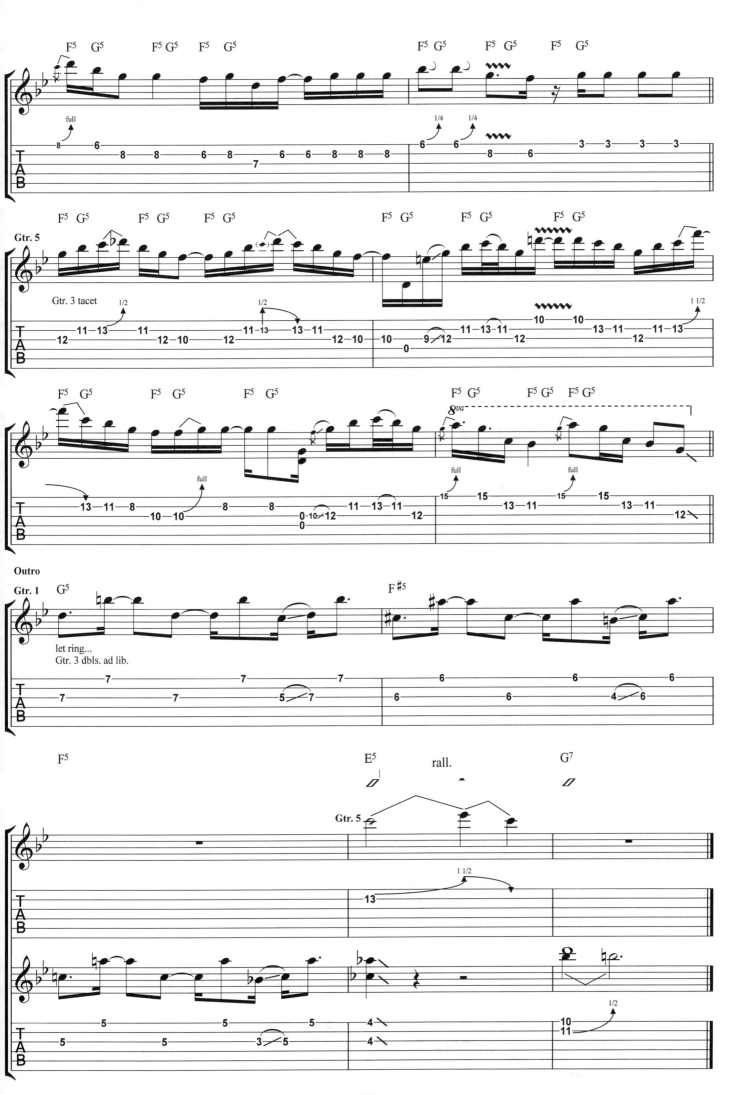

Guitar Tablature Explained

Guitar music can be notated in three different ways: on a musical stave, in tablature, and in rhythm slashes

RHYTHM SLASHES are written above the stave. Strum chords in the rhythm indicated. Round noteheads indicate single notes.

THE MUSICAL STAVE shows pitches and rhythms and is divided by lines into bars. Pitches are named after the first seven letters of the alphabet.

TABLATURE graphically represents the guitar fingerboard. Each horizontal line represents a string, and each number represents a fret.

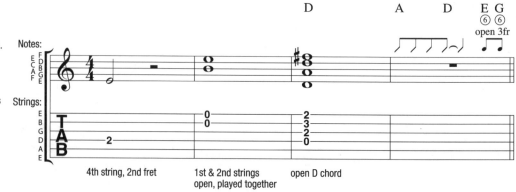

4th string, 2nd fret   1st & 2nd strings open, played together   open D chord

Definitions For Special Guitar Notation

SEMI-TONE BEND: Strike the note and bend up a semi-tone (1/2 step).

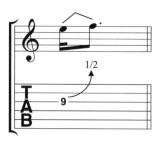

BEND & RELEASE: Strike the note and bend up as indicated, then release back to the original note.

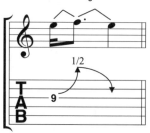

HAMMER-ON: Strike the first note with one finger, then sound the second note (on the same string) with another finger by fretting it without picking.

NATURAL HARMONIC: Strike the note while the fret-hand lightly touches the string directly over the fret indicated.

WHOLE-TONE BEND: Strike the note and bend up a whole-tone (whole step).

COMPOUND BEND & RELEASE: Strike the note and bend up and down in the rhythm indicated.

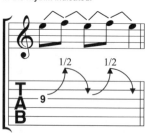

PULL-OFF: Place both fingers on the notes to be sounded, strike the first note and without picking, pull the finger off to sound the second note.

PICK SCRAPE: The edge of the pick is rubbed down (or up) the string, producing a scratchy sound.

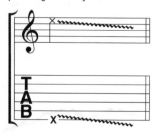

GRACE NOTE BEND: Strike the note and bend as indicated. Play the first note as quickly as possible.

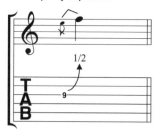

PRE-BEND: Bend the note as indicated, then strike it.

LEGATO SLIDE (GLISS): Strike the first note and then slide the same fret-hand finger up or down to the second note. The second note is not struck.

PALM MUTING: The note is partially muted by the pick hand lightly touching the string(s) just before the bridge.

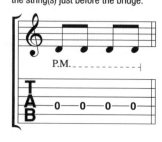

QUARTER-TONE BEND: Strike the note and bend up a 1/4 step.

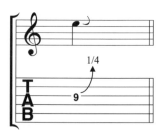

PRE-BEND & RELEASE: Bend the note as indicated. Strike it and release the note back to the original pitch.

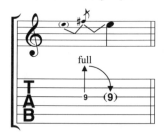

MUFFLED STRINGS: A percussive sound is produced by laying the fret hand across the string(s) without depressing, and striking them with the pick hand.

SHIFT SLIDE (GLISS & RESTRIKE): Same as legato slide, except the second note is struck.

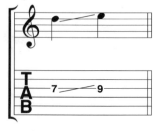

NOTE: The speed of any bend is indicated by the music notation and tempo.

1 2 3 4 5 6 7 8 9